Premier English

for Nigerian Primary Schools

PUPIL'S BOOK **6**

Author
Nick Coates

Advisers
Olubunmi Olabisi Owoeye
Adedayo Olufemi Charles Aderibigbe
Susan Ayeni
Mohammed Bala
Okeke Okocha

MACMILLAN

Contents

Module	Reading and Comprehension	Grammar and Function	Speech	Dictation and Composition	Page
1	**Tourism in Nigeria** An argumentative text	Revision of verb forms (1): the present simple, past simple and present perfect tenses	Class debate Discussion on local tourism	An argumentative essay A local guide for tourists	4
2	**The accident** A modern adventure story	Revision of verb forms (2): the present continuous, past continuous and present perfect continuous tenses	Ask about people and things Ask for and give directions	An informal letter A guided summary of the story	9
3	**Three letters** An informal, semi-formal and formal letter about an accident	Revision of verb forms (3): the past perfect tense	Revision of falling and rising intonation Dialogue	Compare layout and style of informal, semi-formal and formal letters Formal letter to accept an invitation	13
4	**The fire on the hill** A traditional story	Past perfect continuous tense – with *just, already, never*	Speech Act out a story	Opening paragraphs	18
5	**It's the best!** Adverts, bills and receipts	Past perfect simple and continuous tenses contrasted	Revision of fall-rise intonation for enthusiasm Radio advert	Concluding paragraphs A receipt	22
6	**A news report** Report from a newspaper	Reported speech (1): revision and tense changes	Formal speech Role play of an interview	A police report	27
7	**Sports reports** Sports report in a school magazine	Reported speech (2): questions	Formal speech	A sports report An informal letter	31
8	**Water pollution** Letters of complaint and response	Reported speech (3): words of time and place	Speech (of complaint) Class debate	A formal letter of complaint An argumentative essay	35
9	**The gift** A play	Relative pronouns – *what*	Read a play	Write a short play	40
10	**Revision A** Poem: *My hands* Revision quiz	Revision – objective questions	Perform a play Oral picture story	Stories or a poem Report, formal letter or argumentative essay	45
11	**The quarrel** A traditional story about nature	Similes and metaphors	Poem: *Sleep* Confusing words	Link words (of time) A story from a point of view	49
12	**A pronunciation guide** Excerpt from a dictionary Instructions to make a paper plane	Antonyms and synonyms	Recognise phonemes Recognise rhyme	An expository essay	54
13	**Safe water** Expository text and an experiment	*some* and *any* *something, anywhere, nobody*, etc.	Falling and rising intonation with *Wh-* question	Record results of experiments	59
14	**The oceans** Dialogue on oceans and ocean life	Compound nouns	Stress on compound nouns Dialogue	Guided expository essays	64
15	**Health and drugs** Expository text	Prefixes and suffixes	Stress on words with prefixes and suffixes	Guided expository essay Dialogue	68

Module	Reading and Comprehension	Grammar and Function	Speech	Dictation and Composition	Page
16	Finding out about HIV/AIDS Children research the subject	Suffixes and word families	Word stress shifts Discuss/make a wall poster	Informal letter about HIV/AIDS/drugs A report of an accident	72
17	The stonecutter A traditional story	Expressing wishes – I wish I were … . If I were …, I would …	Audience, purpose and style Use appropriate utterances	Audience, purpose and style Informal and formal letters on same topic	77
18	Writing a story Guide to good story writing	Phrasal verbs	Stress with phrasal verbs Discuss a story	Proof reading A story	82
19	Idioms and proverbs A magazine English guide	Idioms	Tongue twisters	A tongue twister A diary entry	86
20	Revision B Poem: Fire Revision quiz	Revision: objective questions	Oral picture story	Picture story Report and diary entry on a fire	90
21	The birthday party Organising a gathering	Gerund and to + infinitive	Organise a party Oral report on plans	Written report on plans Letter (informal) of invitation	94
22	The prize-giving ceremony Report of a presentation ceremony	too/not enough; too and very Intensifiers very, rather, terribly, etc.	Deliver a formal speech Speech at prize-giving ceremony	Write a speech Report of a ceremony	98
23	The twins Traditional story	Comparison of adverbs	Class debate Interview	Argumentative essay (give opinions) Record of interview (dialogue)	102
24	Famous Nigerians Biographies	Conditional forms (revision)	Talk on a famous person Poem: Penfriend	Biography Letter to a penfriend	107
25	A famous African Autobiography of Nelson Mandela	1st conditional with modal verbs 1st conditional with when and unless	Talk about 'Myself' Contrasting consonants	Autobiography Diary entry	111
26	Life at secondary school Dialogue	Question tags (with and without auxiliary verbs in the stem)	Intonation with question tags Interview	Record of interview (dialogue) Informal letter	116
27	Computers Expository text	Passive and active forms (revision)	Poem: Sounds of school Talk on future career	Explain future career plans Formal letter to head teacher	121
28	A letter of condolence Modern story about loss	Quantifiers (revision)	Describe people	Good essay writing Opening paragraphs	126
29	Monkey's heart Traditional story	Revision	Picture story Dramatise a story	Write a short play	131
30	Revision C Poem: Wings Revision quiz	Revision: objective questions	Perform a play Speech Recite a favourite poem	Story, informal letter, formal letter, report or diary entry	136
Appendix: Irregular verbs					140
Word list					142

1 Tourism in Nigeria

A Reading 1

Before reading: Have you ever met any foreign tourists? What do they like to see in Nigeria?

Nigerians welcome foreign tourists to Nigeria. Tourists come to see and enjoy our country. They want to meet us and get to know our culture.

Tourism brings many benefits to a country. Tourists spend a lot of money in the places they visit. They need hotels to stay in. They need restaurants and shops to buy their food in. Also, most of them buy souvenirs and gifts for their families and friends at home.

This creates work for the local people. There are jobs in the hotels and restaurants. Craftsmen and women can make and sell the things the tourists want to buy as souvenirs.

Furthermore, developments for tourists can benefit the local people. Better roads are built so that the tourists can get to their hotels quickly and comfortably. Electricity and telephones are brought into areas that did not have them before. This makes life for local people better as well.

B Comprehension 1

1 Why do foreign tourists come to Nigeria?
2 Where do tourists stay when they visit a country?
3 How does this make work for local people?
4 'Tourism brings many benefits to a country.' This means
  A people like tourists,   B tourism is good for a country,
  C tourism is bad for a country.
5 A 'souvenir' is
  A something people buy to remember a place they visit,
  B a local food,   C something people need at home.
6 What do craftsmen and women do?
7 'Furthermore, developments for tourists can benefit the local people.' This means
  A tourists also give money to Nigerians,   B more tourists need to help Nigerians,
  C another good thing is that changes made for the tourists are also good for Nigerians.
8 What developments are made for tourists?

C Reading 2

Before reading: The text on page 4 explains the advantages of tourism. Can you think of any disadvantages?

There are some disadvantages to tourism. Tourists may not respect our traditions. They might behave badly in our shrines, churches or mosques. If too many people visit one area, they can turn a quiet, beautiful place into a crowded, noisy, dirty one. They produce a lot of traffic and litter. Plants or animals can be killed accidentally.

A lot of the foreign tourists who come to Africa want to see animals. Most countries have special areas called nature reserves or national parks where people can watch animals living in the wild. About ten per cent of Kenya is used for national parks. About one million tourists visit Kenya every year. With so many visitors, the area is polluted. Also, the local hunters cannot hunt and kill the animals any more.

In Nigeria, we have national parks but we have fewer animals than in Kenya. However, we do have many things that foreign tourists like. We have beautiful beaches, a warm sea, lakes and rivers to swim in, rain forest, mountains, small villages and busy cities. Many people are very interested in our long history and rich culture. They like to watch festivals and visit the craft villages to see our traditional cloth being made, or carvers making masks.

In the future, more tourists are likely to visit Nigeria. We must make sure they bring all the advantages but few of the disadvantages.

D Comprehension 2

1 Where might tourists behave badly?
2 What happens if too many people visit the same place?
3 Why do many foreign tourists come to Africa?
4 How many tourists visit Kenya each year?
5 Do you think local hunters in Kenya are happy about tourism?
6 'In Nigeria … we have fewer animals than in Kenya' This means
   A there are more animals in Nigeria than in Kenya,
   B there are more animals in Kenya than in Nigeria,
   C there are the same number of animals in Kenya and Nigeria.
7 'In the future, more tourists are likely to visit Nigeria.' This means
   A in the future, more tourists will come to Nigeria,
   B in the future, more tourists might come to Nigeria,
   C in the future, more tourists can come to Nigeria.
8 Do you think more foreign tourists should come to Nigeria? Why/Why not?

> **Word focus**🔍   **Make sentences with these words:**
> tourism   foreign   advantage   disadvantage   benefit   culture
> souvenir   craft   spend   development   crowded   furthermore

E Grammar

1 Which verb tenses do you know in English?
2 Name the tenses of the underlined verbs (past simple, present simple or present perfect). Then complete the sentences about the uses of the tenses.
   (a) Tourism brings a lot of benefits to Nigeria.
   (b) Over a million tourists visited Kenya last year.
   (c) Many foreign tourists have been to Africa on holiday.
   (i) When we talk about habits or things that are always true, we use the
       _____ tense.
   (ii) When we talk about something that started in the past and is still true in the present, we use the _____ tense.
   (iii) When we talk about events and actions that happened in the past, we use the _____ tense.
3 Write sentences using the correct form of the present simple tense.
     usually/tourists/stay/in hotels   Tourists usually stay in hotels.
   (a) go/I/never/on holiday   (b) sweets/children/usually/like
   (c) Tope/go/to Ghana/every year   (d) always/Deola/parties/enjoy
   (e) Suleiman/near Kano/live

4 Complete the sentences using the verb in the past simple or present perfect tense.

_____ you ever _____ (see) lions?   Have you ever seen lions?

(a) Mum is out. She _____ (go) to work.

(b) She _____ (go) to work ten minutes ago.

(c) My father travels a lot. He _____ (visit) many countries.

(d) He _____ (visit) the USA last month.

(e) I _____ (never/visit) the USA.

(f) Look! It _____ (just/start) to rain.

(g) Tolu _____ (buy) his ticket to Togo yesterday.

(h) Who _____ (win) the football match yesterday?

F Speech

1 Hold a class debate on the motion: 'Tourism is good for Nigeria'.

(a) Work in groups. Prepare all your ideas for the topic.

(b) Listen to your teacher explain how to organise the debate.

- *Proposers:* prepare a speech to propose the motion. Think of all the ideas you can to support it.

- *Opposers:* prepare a speech to oppose the motion. Think of all the ideas you can against it.

- *Rest of class:* think of questions to ask the speakers.

2 Discuss these questions.

(a) What interesting places are there in your area for tourists to see? (mosques, churches, shrines, forests, mountains, rivers, lakes, etc.)

(b) Are there any interesting things for tourists to do? (climb mountains, swim in the sea, etc.)

(c) What is made in your area which tourists can buy? Can they go to see the craftspeople making the things?

(d) Are there any festivals they can see?

(e) Where can tourists stay at night and where can they eat?

G Dictation

Look at the words below. They are all in the dictation you are going to do.
Then listen to your teacher and write the paragraph.

destination	tourists	cultures	religions
spend	crowded	traditional	explore

H Composition

1 Write a composition on the advantages and disadvantages of tourism in Nigeria. You can use the ideas in the texts on pages 4 and 5, and the ideas discussed in the debate.

> You can use some of these phrases.
>
> | | |
> |---|---|
> | *The advantages are ...* | *The disadvantages are ...* |
> | *One of the benefits is ...* | *One of the drawbacks is ...* |
> | *On the one hand, ...* | *On the other hand, ...* |
> | *A positive point is ...* | *A negative point is ...* |
> | *In my opinion, ...* | *To conclude, ...* |

2 Write a guide for tourists in your area.

(a) Complete the form. Use notes: not sentences.

A tourist guide to:
What to do and see:
Places to stay:
Places to eat:
Things to buy:
Other things of interest:

(b) Write the guide. Use about 60 to 100 words. Start:

A visit to _____ can be very enjoyable. Tourists can ...

Fun box

Can you speak to tourists in their own language?
Here is 'thank you' in a few different languages.

French — merci
Chinese — xie xie
German — danke
Hindi — sukria
Japanese — arigato
Spanish — gracias
Swahili — asante

2 The accident

A Reading 1

Before reading: Have you ever seen an accident? What happened?

Zarat was walking home from school last week when there was an accident. She didn't see the accident happen because it was behind her, but she heard it. She quickly ran back and saw that a man had fallen off his bicycle. He was lying on the road. Then she saw that a car had gone off the road. It had gone through a wall into someone's garden.

Tunde ran up just then. He told Zarat that the man on the bicycle was turning across the road when the car hit him. He said that the car was going very fast — too fast for the driver to stop when he saw the cyclist.

The children saw that the cyclist had a broken leg and was bleeding from the head. He didn't speak. They also heard someone groaning in the car. Tunde ran back to school to ask a teacher to telephone for help. Zarat knew that she should not touch the cyclist in case she made the injuries worse. So she sat down next to the man and told him that help was coming.

As Zarat was talking to the man, she smelt petrol. She saw that it was leaking from the car. She was afraid that the petrol might catch fire and the car could explode. She knew that the people had to get out of the car quickly.

B Comprehension 1

1 What was Zarat doing when she heard the accident?
2 Where was the cyclist when Zarat arrived?
3 Where was the car?
4 What had the cyclist been doing when the car hit him?
5 What injuries did the cyclist have?
6 What did Tunde do to help?
7 What did Zarat do to help the cyclist?
8 Why was Zarat afraid when she smelt petrol?

Reading 2

Before reading: What do you think Zarat did next? How could she help the people in the car?

Zarat ran to the car and pulled open the door. The driver was not seriously injured. He had hit his chest against the steering wheel of the car. Zarat told him to get out and run away from the car but the man refused. His son was in the seat next to him. The boy wasn't moving.

Zarat ran around to the other side, opened the door and looked at the injured boy. He was about ten years old. He had had a bang on the head and was unconscious. Zarat tried to pull him out of the car but the boy's leg was stuck. She couldn't move him. She pushed her hands down beside the boy's leg. She felt that his foot was trapped under the seat. Fortunately, it wasn't very tight. Zarat undid the boy's shoelace and was able to pull his foot out of the shoe.
The boy's leg then came free and she pulled him out of the car.

Just then a policeman arrived, took the boy in his arms and ran with him away from the car. Zarat took the driver's hand and helped him to run too.

After that, many people arrived to help. The policeman took Zarat's name and told her that she was a heroine. Zarat felt very proud of herself.

D Comprehension 2

1 Who was in the car?
2 What had happened to the driver in the accident?
3 Why didn't the driver want to leave the car?
4 Why couldn't Zarat pull the boy out of the car?
5 How did Zarat free the boy's leg?
6 Find one word in the whole story which means the following.
   (a) losing blood   (b) giving a low sound of pain
   (c) blow up with a loud noise
   (d) in a very deep sleep because of an accident
   (e) a girl or woman who does something brave

Word focus 🔍

Make sentences with these words:

groan   injury   petrol   explode   bang   steering wheel   unconscious
trap   shoelace   heroine

1 Look.

Continuous verb tenses show the action or event goes on over a period of time. They use part of the verb **be** + the **-ing** form of the main verb.

Present continuous: for actions and events that are happening now.

He **is doing** his homework.

Past continuous: for actions and events that were still continuing at a past time.

Zarat **was** walk**ing** to school when the accident happened.

Present perfect continuous: for actions and events that started in the past but are unfinished up to now.

He **has been** doing his homework since six o'clock.

2 Write *ten* sentences from the table. *Five* sentences will use the present continuous tense and *five* the present simple tense.

The policeman	is writing	to London every week.
	writes	reports about accidents every day.
The pilot	is flying	many patients every day.
	flies	different crops every year.
The farmer	is growing	houses, schools and other buildings.
	grows	a report about the accident.
The builder	is building	a new school at the moment.
	builds	the driver and his son in hospital.
Doctors	are helping	to London at the moment.
	help	cotton this year.

(a) The policeman is writing a report about the accident.

(b) The policeman writes ...

3 Choose the past simple or past continuous tense.

(a) Zarat *walked/was walking* to school when she heard the accident.

(b) Zarat *walked/was walking* to school yesterday.

(c) Last night I *watched/was watching* TV.

(d) I *watched/was watching* TV at eight o'clock last night.

(e) He *had/was having* a shower when he slipped over.

4 Choose the present perfect or present perfect continuous tense.

(a) The cyclist *has broken/has been breaking* his leg.

(b) I *have done/have been doing* my homework for ten minutes.

(c) I *have done/have been doing* my homework. It is finished now.

(d) It *has rained/has been raining* since eight o'clock.

(e) We *have driven/have been driving* for six hours now.

F Speech

1 Imagine you are Zarat or Tunde. You want to know if the boy in the accident is OK. What will you say

(a) to your parents? You want permission to go to the hospital.

(b) to a woman in the street? You want directions to the hospital.

(c) to the man at the entrance to the hospital? You want to know which hospital ward the boy is in. (The boy's name is Sakiru Buhari.)

(d) to the nurse in the hospital ward? You want to know how the boy is.

2 Ask for and give directions. Work in pairs: one is A and one is B, then swap.

A: *Excuse me, can you tell me the way to the hospital, please?*

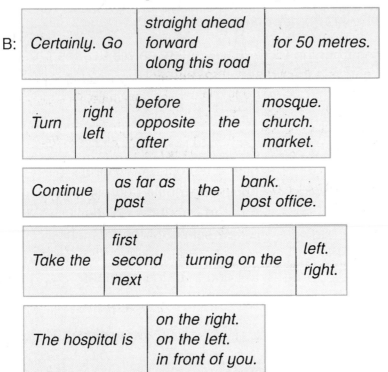

B: Certainly. Go	straight ahead forward along this road	for 50 metres.

Turn	right left	before opposite after	the	mosque. church. market.

Continue	as far as past	the	bank. post office.

Take the	first second next	turning on the	left. right.

The hospital is	on the right. on the left. in front of you.

G Dictation

Look at the words below. They are all in the dictation you are going to do. Then listen to your teacher and write the paragraph.

accident   better   tired   conscious   heroine

H Composition

Write a letter from Zarat to her cousin, Zainab, in the United States. Tell Zainab all about the accident. Zarat and Zainab are about the same age, so this should be a friendly, informal letter.

3 Three letters

A Reading 1

Before reading: Zarat has received two letters. Who are they from?

15 Vermont Avenue,
New York,
2345
USA

18 September 2004

Dear Zarat,

Thanks for your letter – it was great to hear about your adventure. Congratulations! I've been telling all my friends that my cousin's a heroine! If it gets into the newspapers, please send me a copy.

Weren't you afraid when you were trying to free the boy's foot? What would you have done if it had stayed trapped? Would you have taken a knife and cut off his foot?

Hope to see you in the next school holidays. Say hello to your mum and dad for me. See you soon.

Love,
Zainab

Ward 7,
Memorial Hospital,

22 September 2004

Dear Zarat,

My name is Sakiru Buhari and I'm the boy you rescued from the car last week. I want to thank you for saving my life.

I was unconscious so I didn't see you but my father has told me what you did. You were very brave. I think we were very lucky that you were near when we had the accident.

I banged my head when we hit the wall but it's not serious. I'll be going home from hospital tomorrow. My father broke three ribs but he didn't have to stay in hospital. I don't know what happened to the man on the bike - I hope he's all right.

When I'm better I'm going to come to your house to say thank you personally. The policeman gave me your address.

Yours gratefully,
Sakiru Buhari

B Comprehension 1

1 What is Zainab's address?
2 Is her letter formal or informal?
3 Why did Zainab write her letter? Was it to
   A say sorry to Zarat,   B congratulate Zarat,   C invite Zarat to visit her?
4 Where was Sakiru when he wrote his letter?
5 Will he stay there a long time?
6 Is his letter more formal or less formal than Zainab's letter?
7 Why did Sakiru write his letter? Was it to
   A ask Zarat to visit him,   B congratulate Zarat,   C thank Zarat for saving him?
8 'When I'm better I'm going to come to your house to say thank you personally.'
   This means
   A Sakiru will visit Zarat's house himself,   B Sakiru will telephone Zarat,
   C Sakiru will visit Zarat's house with another person.

C Reading 2

Before reading: Who has received the letter on page 15? Who is it from?

D Comprehension 2

1 Is this a formal or informal letter?
2 'It has been brought to my attention …'. This means
   A I saw myself …,   B I have been told …,   C I think it is true … .
3 Why was Zarat correct not to move the cyclist?
4 'She did not hesitate …'. This means
   A she was not afraid,   B she thought carefully,   C She did not waste time.
5 Why does the Chief Inspector want to have a ceremony?
6 When will the ceremony be?
7 Who is the Chief Inspector inviting to the ceremony, apart from Zarat and her family?
8 Why did the Chief Inspector write the letter? Was it to
   A comment on Zarat's behaviour and to invite her and her family to a ceremony,
   B thank Zarat for helping at the accident,   C tell Zarat's family what she did?

Word focus🔍   **Make sentences with these words:**
rescue   save someone's life   personally   gratefully   opportunity
publicise   reporter   suitable

District Police Headquarters
Liberation Avenue

22 September 2004

Alhaji Quadri Abubakar
P.O. Box 273
Abuja

Dear Sir

Re: Road accident on School Road: 15 September

It has been brought to my attention that your daughter, Zarat, was the first to arrive at the scene of a recent accident. I am told that she behaved with intelligence and bravery.

Her decision not to touch the injured cyclist was excellent. It is always possible that moving an injured person will cause more injury. Zarat talked to the man and waited for the ambulance to arrive.

However, when she realised the danger of an explosion caused by petrol, Zarat acted with great speed and bravery. She did not hesitate to enter the car and help the trapped passenger. She had the good sense to remove the boy's shoe to free his trapped leg. She knew there was a chance that the car could catch fire but she still did the right thing. Your daughter is a heroine and you can feel proud to be her parent.

I would like to thank Zarat personally and take the opportunity to publicise what happened. I think it is important that we tell the public when our young people do well. I want to invite you, Zarat and the rest of your family, to come to Police Headquarters on Saturday at 10.00 for a small ceremony. I will also invite some reporters so that they can report the details in their newspapers.

Please let me know if this is suitable for you.

Yours faithfully,

T Oladokun

Chief Inspector Tolu Oladokun

E Grammar

1 Look.

To talk about an earlier past, use the **past perfect tense**. It is made with **had** + the past participle of the verb.

*When Zarat arrived at the scene she saw that a man **had fallen** off his bicycle.*
*Sakiru wrote a letter to Zarat. He **had got** her address from the policeman.*

2 Make questions and answers about the pictures.

1 *Why was the man afraid?*
2 • *He had heard a terrible noise.*
3 • *He had seen a ghost.*
4 • *He had felt a cold hand on his back.*
• *He had been having a bad dream.*

3 Complete these sentences.

(a) I went to bed late last night because I had ...

(b) The house was in a mess because we hadn't ...

(c) Our teacher was pleased with us because ...

4 What is the difference in meaning between these pairs of sentences?

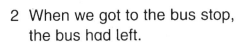

(a) 1 When we got to the bus stop, the bus left.

2 When we got to the bus stop, the bus had left.

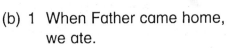

(b) 1 When Father came home, we ate.

2 When Father came home, we had eaten.

5 Choose the correct form of the verb.

(a) Tunde wasn't at home when I arrived. He *went/had gone* out.

(b) Miriam was at home when we arrived, but she *went/had gone* out soon afterwards.

(c) Ugo was late for school yesterday. When she got to the classroom, the lesson *started/had started*.

(d) Ugo was on time today. After she got to the classroom, the lesson *started/had started*.

(e) Johnson didn't play in the last game because he *hurt/had hurt* his leg before the game.

F Speech

1 Read the following in pairs.

Use falling intonation for statements and **Wh-** questions.

My father got a letter this morning.   *Where is your letter?*

Use rising intonation for other questions and to show surprise or enthusiasm.

Are you going?   *Of course!*   *Hi Tunde!*

Zarat: Hi Tunde! Have you heard about the ceremony at the police headquarters?

Tunde: Yes, isn't it great? My father got a letter this morning.

Zarat: So did mine! Are you going?

Tunde: Of course! I wouldn't miss it for the world!

Zarat: There'll be journalists. Do you think they'll take photographs of us?

Tunde: I expect so. Then we'll be in the newspapers!

2 Imagine you are Zarat or Tunde. You meet another friend. Tell them about the letter and the ceremony you have been invited to.

G Dictation

Read the dialogue above carefully again. Then listen to your teacher and write.

H Composition

1 Look at the three letters on pages 13 and 15. Discuss these questions.

(a) What shows you that the first letter is an informal, personal one?

(b) What is different about the way the second letter is written?

(c) The third letter is formal. In what ways is it different from the other two?

2 Write a formal letter from Zarat's father to the Chief Inspector. Thank him for his letter and accept the invitation to the ceremony.

4 The fire on the hill

A Reading 1

Before reading: Look at the picture. What can you see? What do you think the story is about?

Long ago in East Africa, a judge went to a town to settle an argument between a young man and a rich merchant. The young man wanted to marry the merchant's daughter. The merchant had set a test for the young man. He had completed the test and now wanted to marry the girl he loved. However, the merchant said the young man had cheated.

Everyone from the town gathered around to hear the judge find a solution to the problem. First, he asked the headman what had happened. The headman spoke, "Sir, the daughter of this merchant is very beautiful and clever. Many of the young men of this district wanted to marry her. The merchant decided to settle the matter with a test."

The judge thanked the headman. He then asked the merchant to say what test he had set. The merchant answered, "I said that the young man who would go into the lake near the town and stay in the cold water all night could have my daughter for a wife."

The judge turned to the young man and asked to hear his story. The young man spoke, "The girl's name is Ruth and I have loved her for a long time. I know she loves me too but her father won't allow us to marry. When I heard about the test, I decided to stay in the lake all night so that I could marry her. But my mother cried and tried to stop me. She thought the animals that go there at night would kill me."

B Comprehension 1

1 Why did the judge go to the town?
2 Why did the merchant set a test for the young men of the town?
3 What was the test?
4 Did the young man who loved Ruth complete the test?
5 Why didn't the merchant let the young man marry Ruth after the test?
6 Why didn't the young man's mother want him to take the test?

C Reading 2

Before reading: Why did the merchant say the young man cheated? How will the judge solve the problem?

The young man continued, "When night came, I went to the lake and entered the cold water. The merchant sent his servants to a place where they could watch me. My mother followed me and climbed a hill forty paces away from the place where I stood. She made a fire on top of the hill to frighten away the wild animals. I saw the fire, too. I understood that my mother was there. I thought of my mother's love, and that of Ruth, so it was easy for me to stay all night in the icy cold water. When morning came, I stumbled from the lake and went to the merchant's house. But he refused to let me marry Ruth."

There was an angry murmur in the crowd of people. The judge raised his hand and turned again to the merchant. He spoke one word, "Why?"

The rich man said, "There was a fire on a hill forty paces from the lake. It warmed him, and that is why he could stay all night in the water. So he cannot marry my daughter."

"Well," the judge said, "this is a very simple case." He asked for a pot of cold water. Then he told the merchant to walk forty paces from the pot and make a fire. "Now," said the judge to the merchant, "you will wait here until the water is warm. I am going to rest and everyone else can go home."

The merchant saw quickly that the fire could not warm the water. He knew he had lost and fell to his knees. So the young man married the rich man's daughter. They lived happily for many years.

D Comprehension 2

1 Why were the merchant's servants at the lake?
2 What did the young man's mother do?
3 How did the fire on the hill help the young man?
4 'I stumbled from the lake'. This means
   A I ran from the lake,   B I walked with difficulty from the lake,
   C I fell from the lake.
5 'There was an angry murmur in the crowd'. Murmur means
   A a low quiet sound,   B a loud shout,   C a lot of hand-waving.
6 Why did the merchant say the young man had cheated?
7 What did the judge tell the merchant to do?
8 Why did the merchant know that he had lost?

E Grammar

1 Look.

Use the **past perfect continuous tense** to talk about something that continued in an earlier past.

*I **had been running** for two hours when I fell over.*

*It **had been raining** all night so the road was wet.*

The past perfect continuous tense is made with **had** + **been** + VERB+**ing**

I You He, She, It We They	had had not (hadn't)	been	waiting. swimming. standing. sleeping. watching.

2 Complete the sentences. Use the past perfect continuous tense.

(a) The young man was cold because he ... (stand) in the lake all night.

(b) He succeeded in his test because his mother ... (watch) him all night and had lit a fire.

(c) I was wet because I ... (wait) in the rain for an hour.

(d) The dog was wet because it ... (swim) in the river.

(e) My mother ... (not sleep) well for a week before she went to see the doctor.

3 Look.

We often use **just**, **already** and **never** with the past perfect continuous tense.

My friend asked me to go swimming yesterday. I said no, because

• *I had **just** been swimming,* (**just** – a short time before)

• *I had **already** been swimming earlier,* (**already** = done before)

• *I had **never** been swimming and was afraid.* (**never** = not before)

4 Make sentences. Use the words in brackets and the past perfect continuous tense.

It was still raining.   (already/rain/six hours)

It had already been raining for six hours.

(a) I was still walking.   (already/walk/two hours)

(b) They went fishing for the first time.   (never/fish)

(c) They were still looking.   (already/look/three days)

(d) Why was he so tired?   (because/just/run)

(e) Why were you so sleepy this afternoon?   (because/I/just/sleep)

F Speech

1 Imagine you are the young man in the story. The judge has asked you to tell your story. Give your speech to the judge – see pages 18 and 19.

2 Act out the meeting in front of the judge. Work in groups of four.
   • Choose the parts of judge, headman, merchant and young man.
   • Practise reading your parts before you act the story out.

G Dictation

Look at the words below. They are all in the dictation you are going to do.
Then listen to your teacher and write the paragraph.

| judge   court   evidence   accused   jury   innocent   guilty   sentence |
| fine   prison |

H Composition

1 Read the first paragraph of
   (a) the text on tourism on page 4,   (b) the story of 'The accident' on page 9,
   (c) the story of 'The fire on the hill' on page 18.

The opening paragraph of a text should
   • make it clear what the text is about,
   • be interesting or exciting so that the reader wants to read more.

2 Imagine you want to write a composition on 'My school'. Which is the best opening sentence?
   A I attend Premier Primary School.
   B I get up at seven o'clock, have my breakfast and then go to school.
   C The Premier Primary School is the centre of my life, and that of 600 other pupils.

3 Write an opening sentence about 'My school'.

4 Write *two* more sentences to complete the opening paragraph.

The first sentence of a paragraph tells us what the paragraph is about.
The other sentences give examples or supporting information.

5 Write opening paragraphs for the following compositions.
   (a) My home   (b) My family   (c) An accident

5 It's the best!

A Reading 1

Before reading: Look at the adverts below and, as fast as possible, find one advert that

(a) offers you something for free,

(b) wants you to buy something,

(c) tells you about entry to a school,

(d) asks you to apply for a job,

(e) tells you about an event.

A

Children's Book Sale

Reading is fun

Date: 19th–26th November
Time: 8.00 AM to 4:00 PM
Place: ABC House, Century
Shopping Complex, Victoria Island

B

WANTED

1. **Receptionist**
   20–25 years. Must speak good English
2. **Secretaries**
   Diploma or graduate
3. **Manager**
   For a restaurant. 30–40 years

C

CLEAR QUALITY
Brand New GSM Phones
All leading makes
Sale!!
20% Price Drop!!

Prices start from
N8,000

Agents throughout Nigeria
Head Office: Clear Quality Communications   Area 7, Garki-Abuja.   Tel. 09-3491, 0801-992-615

D

STAR COLLEGE, ENUGU
(Day & Boarding School)

Admission in progress

Cambridge 'O' Level & 'A' Level
And transfers into: **JSS I & II, SSS I & II**

Star College
110 Central Avenue, Enugu
0801-245677

E

FREE COMPUTER COURSE
BY MAIL from America

For your *free* course please send
your name and address to:
University Computer School,
Private Mail Bag XX, Ikoyi, Lagos.

B Comprehension 1

1 When is the book sale?
2 What language do you need to speak for the receptionist job?
3 How old should you be to apply for the job as a restaurant manager?
4 How much is the cheapest mobile phone?
5 What numbers can you call to find out more about mobile phones?
6 Where is Star College?
7 Is Star College a primary or a secondary school?
8 What should you do if you want the free computer course?

C Reading 2

Before reading: What is a bill? What is a receipt?

A

Children's Book Sale

ABC House, Century Shopping Complex,
Victoria Island

RECEIPT No: A023

Date: 19 November 2004

Received from Zarat Abubarkar

I x English dictionary	I 500.00
I x The Lion and Olu	150.00
I x Poetry is fun	200.00
TOTAL	**I 850.00**

Received with thanks by: P Egede

B

STAR COLLEGE

110 Central Avenue, Enugu
0801-245677

Date: 5 January 2005

School term bill for: Atinuke Kolawole
To: Mr Gbenga Kolawole

Payment is now due:

Books	I 200.00
After school lessons	I 000.00
Music lessons	I 500.00
School trip	800.00
TOTAL	**4 500.00**

Please make sure that payment reaches us within 14 days of
the date on this bill

D Comprehension 2

1 Look at the receipt (A).
   (a) Who bought these books?   (b) What shop did she buy them from?
   (c) When did she buy them?   (d) How many books did she buy?
   (e) How much did she pay in total?
   (f) Who took her money and gave her the receipt?
2 Look at the bill (B).
   (a) Who is this bill for?   (b) Who has to pay the money?
   (c) Who does Mr Kolawole have to pay?
   (d) How much were the music lessons?
   (e) How much is the total bill for?
   (f) How soon must the bill be paid?

E Grammar

1 Look.

> The **past perfect simple** and **continuous** tenses both talk about an earlier past.
> The **simple** form shows the action was **completed** in the earlier past.
> The **continuous** form shows the action was **continuing** in the earlier past.
>   *She **had waited** for an hour so she went home.*
>   *She **had been waiting** for an hour when he arrived.*

2 Complete these sentences. Choose the best tense of the verb.

(a) He returned the book to the library because he *had read/had been reading* it.

(b) He *had read/had been reading* the book for a week when he lost it.

(c) When Tunde arrived, Zarat *had done/had been doing* her homework. She hadn't finished so she asked Tunde to help.

(d) Mother *had made/had been making* some amala and soup, so I took some.

(e) They *had talked/had been talking* for ten minutes before she saw that he had no shoes on.

(f) They *had talked/had been talking* before about the problem with the phone.

(g) Zarat *had met/had been meeting* Tunde's father before.

3 Read and complete the text using the verbs in the box.

> had been raining   had been walking   had been cutting   had gone
> had read   had been dreaming   had seen

Rebecca woke up and jumped out of bed. She (a)_____ but she wanted to forget the dream as quickly as possible. In the dream she (b)_____ through a dark forest and she (c)_____ something terrible. A man (d)_____ some wood when some wild dogs attacked him. Rebecca knew it was only a dream. She knew it was caused by something she (e)_____ in a story the night before. But she was frightened and wanted her mother.

Rebecca went into her mother's room but her mother (f)_____ out. Rebecca looked out of the window and saw that it was still raining. It (g)_____ since the afternoon of the day before. There were pools of water everywhere. Where could her mother have gone?

F Speech

1 Say the following. They are all from radio adverts.

In adverts, people sound enthusiastic about what they want to sell.
Use the fall-rise intonation

  (a) It's the best!   (b) Clear quality!

  (c) Come to us. You'll be glad you did!

2 Prepare and present a radio advert for one product.

- Work in pairs. Decide on your product.
- Decide what you want to say about it. Make it short but exciting and interesting. You can use a song or a rhyme.
- Practise saying your advert several times.

G Dictation

Look at the words below. They are all in the dictation you are going to do. Then listen to your teacher and write the paragraph.

believe	advert	truth	medicines	doctor	actor

H Composition

1 Read the closing paragraph of
  (a) the text on tourism on page 5,
  (b) the story of 'The accident' on page 10,
  (c) the story of 'The fire on the hill' on page 19.

The closing paragraph of a text should
- finish a story or report (and perhaps point out the moral of the story),
- sum up an argument,
- make it clear that the text is finished.

2 Think about your composition 'My school', which you started in Module 4.
   Which is the best first sentence for the concluding paragraph?
   A After the extra lessons, I go home to watch TV.
   B I feel very proud to be part of the school.
   C The school is good.

3 Write *two* more sentences to complete the closing paragraph.

> The first sentence of a paragraph tells us what the paragraph is about. The other sentences give examples or supporting information.

4 Write closing paragraphs for the following compositions (look back to the opening paragraphs you wrote in Module 4).
   (a) My home   (b) My family   (c) An accident

5 Imagine you work for *Clear Quality Communications*. You have sold a mobile phone to Miss Oluchi Onuoha for N12,000. Complete this receipt.

Clear Quality Communications

Area 7, Garki-Abuja.
09-3491, 0801-992-615

RECEIPT No: CQC 0078

Date: _____

The sum of _____

_____   N   :   K

Received from _____

Being payment for _____

_____

_____

Received by: _____

Fun box

Did you know ...

... a palindrome is a word or sentence that reads the same forwards or backwards? For example,

- dad
- nurses run
- madam
- Was it a cat I saw?

6 A news report

A Reading

Before reading: What can you read about in newspapers?

Do you ever read a newspaper?

B Comprehension

1 What is the headline of the newspaper report on page 28?

2 Is it a report of (a) what happened only, or (b) a report of what happened plus what people said at the ceremony?

3 '... he was congratulated for his quick thinking.' This means
   A he was told quickly that he did well,
   B he was told he did well to make a decision quickly,
   C he was told off because he made a decision too quickly.

4 'The Chief Inspector was full of praise for the two children.' This means
   A the Chief Inspector said the two children did very well,
   B the Chief Inspector was sorry for the two children,
   C the Chief Inspector gave the two children good advice.

5 '...they kept their heads.' This means
   A they didn't do anything silly,   B they held on to their heads,
   C they talked to each other.

6 '...to comfort the injured cyclist.' This means
   A to give medicine and other help to the injured cyclist,
   B to give the injured cyclist a cushion,
   C to make the injured cyclist feel better.

7 '...things took a turn for the worse.' This means
   A things started to turn in circles,   B some help arrived,
   C there were more problems.

8 Why did Yusuf Buhari attend the ceremony?

9 What happened to Mr Buhari after the ceremony?

10 Why did the police arrest him?

Word focus   **Make sentences with these words and phrases:**
dramatic   out of breath   full of praise   keep your head   give comfort to
a turn for the worse   arrest

SCHOOLCHILDREN IN DRAMATIC RESCUE

She is a heroine! Ten-year-old Zarat Abubakar recently helped to rescue a father and son after a road accident.

"She is a brave girl and all Nigerians can feel proud of her," said Chief Inspector Tolu Oladokun.

Zarat was walking home from school two weeks ago when she heard a loud noise behind her.

"When I turned around, I saw a cyclist lying in the road and the back of a car," said Zarat. She was speaking at a ceremony at Police Headquarters yesterday.

"I ran back and went to take care of the cyclist. I decided not to touch him. Then my friend Tunde arrived."

Tunde Adegoke was also at the ceremony yesterday and he was congratulated for his quick thinking. The ten-year-old pupil of the local primary school ran back one hundred metres to the school and found a teacher.

"When I arrived at the school I was out of breath and couldn't talk. The teacher got angry with me but then I explained. She called the police," Tunde told reporters yesterday.

The Chief Inspector was full of praise for the two children. "They did exactly the right thing. They looked at the situation, they didn't panic and they kept their heads. Then one went for help while the other stayed to comfort the injured cyclist. They did not try to pull him off the road because that could have made his injury worse."

But at this point things took a turn for the worse.

Zarat continues the story, "I was sitting on the road talking to the injured cyclist when I smelt petrol. I knew at once that it was coming from the car and that it might catch fire. I also knew that there were people still in the car."

The brave young pupil then tried to get the driver and his passenger out of the car. However, she discovered that the passenger, 11-year-old Sakiru Buhari, couldn't move. She pulled the boy's shoe off and managed to free his leg. She was then able to help the driver and the boy to safety.

"Zarat is a true heroine," said Oladokun. "There are not many adults brave enough to risk their lives in the way that Zarat did."

The driver of the car, Yusuf Buhari, also attended the ceremony with Sakiru. They were there to thank Zarat for her help.

However, Mr Buhari had a surprise when the police arrested him after the ceremony. They said he had been driving too fast.

Also attending the ceremony were the proud parents of Zarat and Tunde.

C Grammar

1 Play the reporting game in groups of three. Decide who is A, B and C.

- A chooses one sentence below and whispers it to B. C must not hear.

> I like fufu and soup.   I'd like some fufu and soup.
> I don't like fufu and soup.   Do you like fufu and soup?

- B reports to C what A said. B must use reported speech (*A said ...,* or *A asked if ...*) and whisper it so that A cannot hear.
- C writes down what B said.
- All read C's sentence. Has A's sentence been reported correctly?

2 Look.

Reported speech: when we report the words someone said, we usually change the verb tense. It moves one step back in time.

Direct speech	Reported speech
*"I often **swim**."* (present simple)	*He said he often **swam**.* (past simple)
*"He **is sleeping**."* (present continuous)	*He said he **was sleeping**.* (past continuous)
*"She **went** to school."* (past simple)	*He said she **had gone** to school.* (past perfect simple)
*"I **was eating**."* (past continuous)	*He said he **had been eating**.* (past perfect continuous)
*"I **have seen** the film."* (present perfect)	*She said she **had seen** the film.* (past perfect)
*"I **will go** with you."* (**will**)	*He said he **would go** with me.* (**would**)
*"I **can swim**."* (**can**)	*She said she **could swim**.* (**could**)

3 Put the sentences in reported speech.

"She is a brave girl," said Chief Inspector Oladokun.

Chief Inspector Oladokun said she was a brave girl.

(a) He said, "All Nigerians can feel proud of Zarat."

(b) Zarat said, "I saw a cyclist lying in the road."

(c) Tunde said, "When I arrived I was out of breath."

(d) "I will stay with the cyclist," said Zarat.

(e) The Chief Inspector said, " They did exactly the right thing."

(f) Zarat said, "I was sitting on the road when I smelt petrol."

(g) The policeman said to Mr Buhari, "You are under arrest."

D Speech

1 Act out an interview between Zarat and a reporter at the ceremony. The reporter wants to know what happened in order to write a newspaper report. Work in pairs.

2 Imagine you are Chief Inspector Oladokun. Prepare a speech to welcome the guests to the ceremony and praise Zarat and Tunde. Your teacher will help you.

E Dictation

Look at the words below. They are all in the dictation you are going to do.
Then listen to your teacher and write the paragraph.

journalist   reporter   newspaper   magazines   inform   public   editor   headline

F Composition

Copy and complete the police report about the accident.

In a report, use only facts. Say what happened, not what you think about it.

Complete the first part with information from the box. Then think of words to fill the gaps in the 'Description of incident'.

10 September, 20__   Road accident   head injury (unconscious)
Zarat Abubakar and Tunde Adegoke   broken ribs

Police Incident Report

Type of incident: Date:

Details of any injuries: Cyclist: broken leg and cut head, Car driver:
Car passenger:

Names of witnesses:

Description of incident: A blue Toyota Corolla, number XTY 765, was travelling north along School Road. The driver was Mr (a) ... . The (b) ... was travelling very fast.
    A cyclist, Mr Chinedu Uchendu, was (c) ... in the same direction. He turned across the (d) ... without looking. The driver of the Corolla could not (e) ... in time. The cyclist was knocked off his (f)   The car left the road and hit a wall.
    Zarat Abubakar, a 10-year-old schoolgirl, arrived first on the scene. She tried to comfort the (g) ... but did not move him. Tunde Adegoke, a schoolboy of 10 years, arrived and then ran to the (h) ... to call for help.
    Zarat noticed the smell of (i) ... from the crashed car. She discovered that the car passenger, Sakiru Buhari (aged 11), was trapped in the car. She managed to release his (j) ... and she then pulled him from the car. At this point, I arrived and helped everyone away from the car.   *Reporting officer:*   Lanre Kayode

---

7 Sports reports

A Reading 1

Before reading: What is your favourite athletic event? Who are the best athletes in your class?

Sports Day: a report by Musa Sadiq

Sports Day at Premier Primary School this year was the biggest and best ever held by the school. The four houses, Green, Yellow, Red and Blue, all competed in many athletic events. These included the 100m, 200m, 400m, 800m, hurdles, 4 x 100m relay, high jump and long jump.

100 metres The 100m race was very exciting this year. Many children ran personal bests, including Tunde Adegoke who won the boys' 100m for Blue house. In the girls' race, Ugo Ukpai ran like a cheetah from the start to give Yellow house its first gold medal.

200 metres In the 200m, Adeda Obalana gained the first win for Green house by beating Ugo Oruche. Ugo was just a second behind her. In the 200m for boys it was Tunde Adegoke again who took first place.

110 metres hurdles Sikiru Ahmed won the 110m hurdles gold medal for Yellow house. He ran quickly and smoothly over the hurdles. It was an unlucky day for Bashiru Adams of Red house as he fell over the second hurdle. He twisted his ankle. Sola Johnson was an easy winner in the girls' race. When she heard, "On your marks, get set, go!" she took off and flew fast over the hurdles. She reached the finishing line several seconds ahead of all her rivals.

B Comprehension 1

1 Who wrote this report?
2 'Many children ran personal bests'. This means
   A many children ran faster than they had ever done before,
   B many children ran better than their friends,
   C many children were very good and ran fast.
3 Which phrase tells you that Ugo Ukpai ran very fast?
4 What happened to Bashiru Adams?

5 Complete the table with the names of the winners of each event.

	100 metres	200 metres	110 metres hurdles
Boys			
Girls			

C Reading 2

Before reading: Which house do you think was the winner at the Sports Day?

Long jump In the long jump, Bintu Ahmed made a poor final jump. She took off 10 cm behind the take-off board. However, she still took first place because her main rival's foot went over the board and produced a 'no-jump'. Sam Okon came first in the boys' long jump.

High jump In the girls' high jump, there was a fascinating competition between four girls. The bar had to be moved higher. The first three contestants then all knocked off the bar. The final contestant, Sade Akanji, ran up. She kicked her legs up and over the bar to win the gold medal for Yellow house. The boys did not do so well as the girls in this competition. Audu Sulaiman won but he did not reach the same height as Sade Akanji.

4 x 100 metres relay The most exciting races of the day were the 4 x 100m relays. The two fastest girls in the school both ran last legs of the girls' race. Ugo ran a fantastic final 30 metres to overtake Adeda near the line. This earned Yellow house a victory. In the boys' relay, it was an unlucky day for Red house as Leye Adelaja, who ran the third leg, dropped the baton when he tried to pass it to Fola Bello. Blue house 4 x 100m relay team came first because they all ran well and their baton change was smooth.

After the last race, the results were announced. Yellow house was named the winner. All the team members danced round the school with their trophy.

The day was a great success. In her speech closing the event, the headmistress announced that four girls and four boys from the school will be chosen to represent the school in the State Primary School Games next month.

D Comprehension 2

1 Who were better at the high jump, the boys or the girls?
2 Who crossed the line first in the girls' 4 x 100 metres relay?
3 What did Leye Adelaja do?
4 Complete the table with the names of the winners of each event.

	Long jump	High jump	4 x 100 metres relay
Boys			
Girls			

5 Which team won the trophy?
6 Who gave a speech at the end of the event?

Word focus

Make sentences with these words:
athletics   hurdles   relay   baton   beat   gain   rival   overtake   trophy

E Grammar

1 Look.

To put a question into reported speech we often have to change the word order.
The sentence is now a report, not a question.

"Who won the high jump?"	Chike asked who won the high jump.
"How are you?"	She asked how I was.
"Are you ready?"	The teacher asked if I was ready.
"Is this yours?"	Mummy asked if it was mine.

Note the changes when we report a question.
- The verb tense changes.
- Pronouns may change.
- Word order may change.
- Use **if** when a **Yes/No question** is reported.

2 A policeman asked Tunde some questions after the road accident. Tunde told
Ugo what the policeman asked. What did Tunde say?

"What is your name?"   He asked me what my name was.

(a) "Where do you live?"
(b) "Which school do you go to?"
(c) "What did you see?"
(d) "How fast was the car going?"
(e) "What was the cyclist doing?"
(f) "Why did you run to the school?"

3 Report these questions.

Zarat asked, "Tunde, are you hungry?"

Zarat asked Tunde if he was hungry.

(a) Tunde asked Zarat, "Do you want a drink?"

(b) "Mum, did you see me running?" asked Ugo.

(c) Chi wanted to know, "Ugo, do you enjoy running?"

(d) "Tunde," asked Mother, "did you win your race?"

(e) The policeman asked Zarat, "Is this your bicycle?"

(f) "Mr Buhari, do you have a driving licence?" asked the policeman.

4 (a) Act out an interview. Work in pairs.

- Imagine one of you is a journalist, and the other one is Tunde Adegoke or Ugo Oruche.
- Ask and answer *three* questions about the Sports Day.

(b) Work together to report the questions and answers.

F Speech

Imagine you are the Guest of Honour at the Sports Day. It is your job to give a speech and present the medals and trophies.

- Prepare your speech. Start:

  The principal, headmistress and staff of Premier Primary School, honoured guests, parents and pupils; thank you for inviting me to this happy occasion.

- Practise your speech before you give it.

G Dictation

Look at the words below. They are all in the dictation you are going to do.
Then listen to your teacher and write the paragraph.

athletes	compete	Olympic Games	honour	represent	gold	silver
bronze						

H Composition

1 Write a report of your last school Sports Day. Describe what the events were and who won. Give some details of the most exciting races and events.

2 Write a letter to a friend about what you did in the last school Sports Day. This is an informal letter and you can give your opinions and thoughts as well as explain what happened.

8 Water pollution

A Reading 1

Before reading: What is pollution? Give some examples of pollution.

Alhaji Ibrahim Hassan
17, Binta Road
Kano

2nd February 2005

The Director
Department of Environmental Health
Kano State Secretariat
Kano

Dear Sir,

Polluted Water

I wish to complain about the stream that flows through Badam Farm near my home. The stream has become dirtier and more polluted over the last few months.

There are two major causes of this pollution. The first is that people working nearby throw their rubbish into the stream. Secondly, farming chemicals run into it. It is a small, slow stream so the harmful chemicals and rubbish are building up. This polluted stream also provides ideal conditions for flies and other insects which can cause health problems. It is also harming wildlife. We have not seen any fish in the stream or any frogs beside it for some time.

Suitable action should be taken soon. If not, the stream will become a serious health problem. I would appreciate your immediate attention in dealing with this problem.

Yours faithfully,

Ibrahim Hassan

Ibrahim Hassan (Alhaji)

B Comprehension 1

1 Is this a formal or informal letter?
2 Who is it to?
3 What is the heading?
4 Who is it from?
5 'This polluted stream also provides ideal conditions for flies ...'. This means
   A the dirty stream is killing flies,   B flies like the dirty stream,
   C flies are making the stream dirty.
6 What do you think has happened to the fish and frogs?

7 'I would appreciate your immediate attention in dealing with this problem.'
This means
A Please look at the stream soon,
B Please think about this pollution at some time,
C Please do something quickly about this pollution.

8 Did Alhaji Hassan write this letter to
A complain,   B congratulate someone,   C ask for help?

C Reading 2

Before reading: What do you think the Director of Environmental Health will do about the problem?

The Office of the Director
Department of Environmental Health
Kano State Secretariat
Kano
19th February 2005

Our Ref: OTM 002847
Alhaji Ibrahim Hassan
17, Binta Road
Kano
Kano State

Dear Alhaji Hassan,

Re: Polluted Stream

Thank you for your letter of 2nd February 2005. We have looked into the matter and we have taken immediate action. On 26th February 2005, scientists will visit the area to take samples of the water which they will test for pollution. When the samples have been tested, our workers will clean the stream and tidy up the surrounding areas.

We have written to the owners of Badam Farm to request that they take care to prevent chemicals from entering the stream. They have agreed to do this.

After we have completed the clean-up, we will test the water from the stream regularly to make sure it is clean. The scientists are confident that the wildlife will return gradually.

I would like to take this opportunity to thank you for reporting the pollution. We are working as hard as possible to make sure everything returns to how it should be. The more quickly we sort the problems out, the better it will be for everybody and the environment.

Yours sincerely,

Dr Sodiq Aliyu
The Director of Environmental Health

D Comprehension 2

1 What is the job of the person who wrote this letter?
2 What will happen on 26 February?
3 What have the owners of Badam Farm agreed to do?
4 What will happen after the stream has been cleaned?
5 'The scientists are confident that the local wildlife will return gradually.' This means
   A the scientists think the fish and frogs will come back quickly,
   B the scientists think the fish and frogs will come back slowly,
   C the scientists think the fish and frogs will not come back.
6 Do you think Alhaji Hassan will be pleased with this letter? Why/Why not?

> **Word focus** 🔍 **Make sentences with these words:**
> complain   flow   chemicals   harm   conditions   deal   sample
> surrounding   request   regularly   confident   gradually

E Grammar

1 Look.

> When we report what someone said we sometimes have to change words like
> **now, today, here, this**. This is because the time and place have now changed.
> *The scientist agreed, "**This** stream is polluted **today**."*
> *The scientist agreed **that** stream was polluted **that** day.*

2 Match the direct and reported speech time and place words.

Direct speech	Reported speech
(a) now	(i) the day before
(b) today	(ii) that
(c) tomorrow	(iii) that night
(d) yesterday	(iv) the next day
(e) tonight	(v) there
(f) next week	(vi) the following week
(g) here	(vii) then
(h) this	(viii) that day

(a) now, (vii) then

3 Copy and complete these reported sentences.

"I'll pay you tomorrow."   He said he would pay me <u>the next day</u>.

(a) "I'll phone you tonight."   He said he would phone me _____.

(b) "I'm going now."   She said she was going _____.

(c) "We're on holiday today."   They said they were on holiday _____.

(d) "Do you want to go shopping next week?"
    She asked if I wanted to go shopping _____.

(e) "I'll meet you here at six o'clock."
    He said he would meet me _____ at six o'clock.

(f) "Did you do your homework last night?"
    She asked if I had done my homework _____.

4 Report what a friend told you when you met her last year in Calabar.

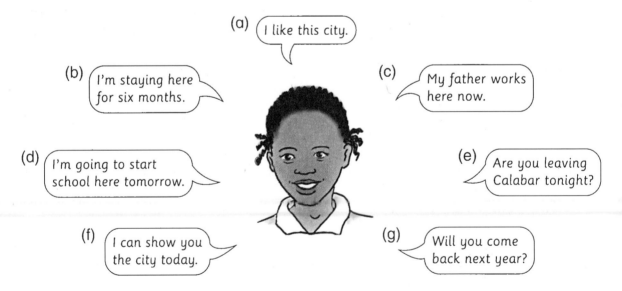

(a) (I like this city.)

(b) (I'm staying here for six months.)

(c) (My father works here now.)

(d) (I'm going to start school here tomorrow.)

(e) (Are you leaving Calabar tonight?)

(f) (I can show you the city today.)

(g) (Will you come back next year?)

(a) She said she liked that city.

F Speech

1 Imagine you are Alhaji Ibrahim Hassan at a public meeting. Give a speech to make a complaint about the stream that flows near your home. Use the information in the letter on page 35. Start:

> *Mr Chairman, ladies and gentlemen; I would like to complain about the stream that flows ...*

2 Hold a class debate on the motion, 'The farmer is more important for our country than the teacher'.

   (a) Work in groups. Prepare all your ideas for the topic.

   (b) Listen to your teacher explain how to organise the debate.
- *Proposers:* prepare a speech to propose the motion. Think of all the ideas you can to support it.
- *Opposers:* prepare a speech to oppose the motion. Think of all the ideas you can against it.
- *Rest of class:* think of questions to ask the speakers.

G Dictation

Look at the words below. They are all in the dictation you are going to do. Then listen to your teacher and write the paragraph.

| complain | respected | education | farmer | teacher | engineer | businessman |

H Composition

1 Imagine the water in your school is dirty and smelly. Write a letter of complaint to the Director of the State Water Corporation. Use the letter on page 35 as a guide.

> You can use some of these phrases.
> *I wish to complain about ...*
> *Suitable action should be taken soon. If not, ...*
> *I would appreciate your immediate attention in dealing with this problem.*

2 Write a composition to discuss the question, 'Which is the more important career, farming or teaching?'
- Decide which career you think is more important.
- Use some of the points from the debate.

> You can use some of the following phrases:
> *My first point is ...*   *Secondly, ...*   *Another point is that ...*
> *Furthermore ...*   *Finally, ...*   *To conclude ...*   *To sum up ...*
> *In my opinion ...*

9 The gift

A Reading 1

Before reading: What is a play? What are characters and a scene?

Characters: *Tunde*, a boy of 11 years old   *Mother*

Mrs Oranugo, a family friend   *Father*

SCENE 1

A living room. There are two doors out of the room. On the left is the front door to the road. The other, on the right, goes to the back of the house. Mother and Father are watching TV. Tunde is walking around anxiously. It is dark outside.

Mother: Tunde, it's time you went to bed.

Tunde: Not yet, Mum. I think Mrs Oranugo will still come.

Mother: That's wishful thinking, my dear. It's too late now.

Father: Well, the traffic was bad on my way back from the office. Who knows? Maybe, she's stuck in traffic.

[Slowly and reluctantly, Tunde walks towards the right door.]

Tunde: Goodnight.

[The doorbell rings. Tunde races to open the front door.]

Tunde: I'll get it!

[Mother and Father laugh quietly and stand up. Tunde opens the door. Mrs Oranugo is standing holding a large package wrapped in coloured paper.]

Mrs O: Hello, Tunde, how are you?

[Tunde stares at the package.]

Tunde: Hello, Ma. I'm fine, thank you.

[Tunde turns to his parents excitedly.]

Tunde: Mum! Dad! Mrs Oranugo's here.

40

Mother: Ah, Mrs Oranugo, thank you for coming.

Father: Good evening, Mrs Oranugo.

Mrs O: Good evening. Sorry I'm this late but I was in a traffic jam.

[She hands over the package to Mother. Tunde is so excited he grabs it from Mother.]

Mother: Since you phoned, Tunde's been too excited to think or talk about anything else.

Mrs O: I can understand. Well, it's late. I have to get home.

Father: Thanks for bringing the gift all the way from London.

Mrs O: It's my pleasure. I hope it's something Tunde likes.

[Mother and Father walk to the front door with Mrs Oranugo to see her off. Meanwhile Tunde rips open the paper from the package. He looks inside and throws up his arms in excitement.]

Tunde: Wow!

B Comprehension 1

1   How many characters are present at the beginning of Scene 1?

2   What time of day is it?

3   'That's wishful thinking'. 'Wishful thinking' means
   A you don't really believe something,
   B you believe something because you want to,
   C you believe one thing but say something else.

4   'Tunde races to open the front door.' He does this
   A because he's excited,
   B because he's afraid,
   C because he's tired.

5   Why does Mrs Oranugo arrive so late?

6   'Tunde's been too excited to think or talk about anything else.' This means
   A Tunde has not talked because he has been so excited,
   B Tunde has not talked about Mrs Oranugo and the gift at all,
   C Tunde has talked only about Mrs Oranugo and the gift.

7   Why does Mrs Oranugo leave so soon?

8   Do you think Tunde likes what is inside the package? Why/Why not?

C Reading 2

Before reading: What do you think the gift is?

SCENE 2

The same living room. Mrs Oranugo has gone. Mother and Father are standing watching as Tunde takes a pair of roller blades out of the wrapping paper.

Tunde: Mum! Dad! Roller blades! I love them! I've always wanted some.
   [He quickly puts them on.]

Mother:	They're lovely.
Father:	Yes, they are. That's very kind of Uncle Dayo. They must have been expensive.
	[Tunde stands up with the blades on. He walks unsteadily and falls back on the sofa.]
Father:	Careful, let me hold your hands.
Tunde:	I can do it. Leave me. Let go, Dad. I can do it.
Father:	Are you sure?
Tunde:	Yes. I'm positive.
Mother:	Careful.
	[Tunde pushes himself across the floor. He goes faster than he expected and doesn't know how to stop. He crashes into a chair and flies over it. He cries out in pain. His parents run to help him.]
Tunde:	Ow! I've hurt myself.
Father:	He's grazed his knees and they're bleeding.
Mother:	I didn't know roller blades were this dangerous.
Father:	They're not really. He needs to practise but we have to buy him a helmet, kneepads, elbow pads and wrist guards before he can use the roller blades safely.
	[Mother removes the roller blades as Father cleans blood off Tunde's knees.]
Mother:	Don't wear them again until we buy the safety equipment.
Tunde:	When will that be?
Father:	I'll get them tomorrow.

D Comprehension 2

1 What is the gift?
2 Does Tunde already have some roller blades?
3 Who sent the gift?
4 Does Tunde think he can use the roller blades well?
5 Does Tunde know how to use the roller blades well?
6 What happens when he uses them for the first time?
7 What injury does Tunde get in the accident?
8 What safety equipment does Tunde need?

Word focus

Make sentences with these words and phrases:

wishful thinking   reluctantly   package   wrap   grab   unsteadily   graze

42

E Grammar

1 Look.

Use **what** as a relative pronoun to mean 'the thing that' or 'anything that'.
*Tunde's uncle gave him **what** he wanted.*
***What** Tunde did on the roller blades was dangerous.*

2 Make sentences.

(a) The shop didn't have		(i) I bought.
(b) I want to have		(ii) happened to Tunde?
(c) My father always says	what	(iii) I wanted.
(d) I'll pay for		(iv) you have.
(e) Did you hear about		(v) he thinks.

3 Change the sentences. Use **what**.

> The thing they bought was expensive.
> What they bought was expensive.

(a) Tell me the thing that you want.

(b) You can have anything that you need.

(c) The thing that I need is a drink.

(d) The thing I forgot was my Maths book.

(e) I'm sorry about the thing that happened to Tunde.

4 Complete the sentence about what you need.

> What I need is a helmet, kneepads, elbow pads and some wrist guards.

What I need is ...

5 Complete the sentences. Use **who**, **which**, **where**, **when** or **what**.

(a) Tunde received a gift _____ made him very happy.

(b) The uncle _____ sent the gift lives in London.

(c) London is a city _____ there are many shops.

(d) Thank you, that's _____ I wanted.

(e) I met a girl _____ knows your sister.

(f) I remember the day _____ we first met.

(g) I did _____ I could.

(h) Our teacher told us something _____ made us laugh.

(i) Shandam is the place _____ my father was born.

(j) We went to Abuja at a time _____ there was an international meeting.

F Speech

1 Read the play on pages 40 to 42. Work in groups of five.
   (a) Decide who will read the words of Tunde, Father, Mother and Mrs Oranugo. One of you will read the stage directions.

Stage directions tell you what the people do, or what happens, in a play.
The words the actors say are called the **dialogue**.

   (b) Practise reading. Work hard to use correct intonation.
2 Act out the play.
   (a) This time one of you is the director.

The **director** in a play, or film, tell the actors what to do.

   Your director should tell the actors where to stand and what to do.
   (b) Rehearse the play several times.

G Dictation

Look at the words below. They are all in the dictation you are going to do.
Then listen to your teacher and write the paragraph.

| drama | perform | stage | theatre | audience | actor | director | rehearsal |

H Composition

Write a short play about an accident.
   (a) First, decide on a plot.

The **plot** of a story, play or film is what happens in the story, play or film.

   Think about answers to these questions:
   Who has the accident?   What is the cause of the accident?
   What sort of accident?   What is the result?
   How serious is the accident?
   (b) Write a list of the **characters** in your play.
   (c) Write a short description of the **scene**.
   (d) Write the **dialogue** and **stage directions**.

Fun box

Did you know ...

... frogs never stop growing? The older they get, the bigger they get.

A Reading

My hands *by* Jo Peters

Think of all my hands can do,
pick up a pin and do up a shoe,
they can help, they can hurt too,
or paint a summer sky bright blue.

They can throw and they can catch.
They clap the team that wins the match.
If I'm rough my hands can scratch.
If I'm rude my hands can snatch.

Gently, gently they can stroke,
carefully carry a glass of Coke,
tickle my best friend for a joke,
but I won't let them nip or poke.

My hands give and my hands take.
With Gran they bake a yummy cake.
They can mend but they can break.
Think of music hands can make.

B Comprehension

1 The poem lists many things that hands can do. List *six* of the good things and *three* of the bad things hands can do.

2 List all the rhyming words.

do - shoe - _____ - _____   catch - _____ - _____ - _____

stroke - _____ - _____ - _____   take - _____ - _____ - _____

3 Match words from the poem to their meanings.

scratch   (a) To rub gently with a hand, particularly an animal.

snatch   (b) To repair, to make something broken work again.

stroke   (c) To touch lightly to make someone laugh.

tickle   (d) To hurt someone by moving fingernails across their skin.

nip   (e) To push a finger or something hard into someone.

poke   (f) To grab, to take something rudely.

mend   (g) To squeeze someone's skin between two fingers.

4 Make sentences using the words for a to g above.

5 Recite the poem.

C Reading quiz

1 Find the answers in the Reading texts from Modules 1 to 9.

(a) Name *five* of the things tourists like to see or do in Nigeria.

(b) What injuries did the cyclist who was knocked off his bike suffer?

(c) What was Zarat doing when she smelt petrol from the car?

(d) What did Zarat have to do to free the boy's leg?

(e) What was the name of the boy trapped in the car?

(f) What was the date of the road accident?

(g) Where will the free computer course come from?

(h) How much does Mr Gbenga Kolawole have to pay for Atinuke's school trip?

(i) Which race did Sola Johnson win?

(j) Name one of the causes of pollution to the stream near Badam Farm.

2 Write *ten* questions of your own about the Reading texts from Modules 1 to 9.

3 Ask your questions.

Word focus

Make sentences with these words:

arrest   benefit   complain   honour   murmur   praise   receipt
souvenir   stumble   trophy

D Grammar

Complete the sentences. Choose the word or group of words that best fills the gap.

1 Many people _____ our school last year.

   A have visited   B are visiting   C visited

   D had visited   E visits

2 Have you ever _____ a hippopotamus?

   A saw   B seen   C seed

   D see   E sawn

3 My father is out. He _____ to the bank.

   A go   B had gone   C has been going

   D has gone   E has been

4 They _____ to the radio at nine o'clock last night.

   A were listening   B are listening   C listened

   D have listened   E listen

5 I _____ an accident on the way to school.

  A was having   B are having   C have been having

  D had   E have

6 It _____ since three o'clock.

  A rained   B rains   C has rained

  D was raining   E has been raining

7 I was late for school. When I arrived at the bus stop the bus _____.

  A left   B had been left   C leaves

  D is left   E had left

8 I can't play football tomorrow because I _____ my leg last week.

  A hurt   B had hurt   C will hurt

  D hurts   E was hurting

9 I _____ our new teacher before she started teaching us.

  A was seeing   B seen   C saw

  D had seen   E had been seeing

10 We _____ for five minutes when the taxi arrived.

  A were talking   B had talked   C had been talking

  D talked   E are talking

11 "I'll see you next week."

  She said she _____ me the following week.

  A will see   B would see   C can see

  D are seeing   E see

12 "How are you?" Oby asked me how _____

  A I was   B was I   C you are

  D are you   E I were

13 "Do you want a drink?" He asked me _____ a drink.

  A I wanted   B if I want   C want you

  D if I wanted   E I want

14 "We'll do it tomorrow." He said they would do it _____.

  A the next day   B later   C another day

  D next week   E then

15 Tell me _____ you want.

  A who   B which   C that

  D when   E what

E Speech

1 Perform the play you wrote in Module 9.

2 Look at the pictures and sentences. Tell the story.

Many young men loved Ruth.

Her father set a test.

The young man stood in the river all night.

His mother lit a fire.

He completed the test but Ruth's father said he had cheated.

A judge came to settle the argument.

F Dictation

Look at these words. Then listen to your teacher and write the paragraph.

continent   thousand   coastline   desert   mountain   savannah   language

G Composition

1 Write *one* of the following.
   - The story of 'The fire on the hill' that you told in Speech above.
   - The opening and closing paragraphs of a story about your hands.
   - A poem called 'My feet'.

2 Write *one* of the following:
   - The judge's report on the meeting from 'The fire on the hill'.
   - A formal letter from the young man to Ruth's father to complain when he said you had cheated.
   - A composition to answer: Which are more important, hands or feet?

48

11 The quarrel

A Reading 1

Before reading: Look at the picture. What do you think the people are discussing?

Once, not so long ago, there was a village which was famous for its beautiful trees. The trees were huge and had very wide branches with many leaves. They created a deep, comfortable shade. In the hot afternoons, the people of the village sat under them to rest and to talk.

The trees were also popular with birds. Many made their nests in the branches. Unfortunately, this caused a problem. Although it was a cool place to sit, sometimes the people couldn't talk there because of the singing and calling of so many birds.

One day, some of the village elders suggested that all the birds should be killed. A great quarrel began in the village. Some supported the suggestion and some opposed it.

One wise man spoke about nature. He said that all creatures are part of nature, and everything has its part to play. "If you kill the gecko in your hut because he makes a noise at night, won't the mosquito live longer and make more noise in your ear? If we kill the birds, we will all have to pay the price one day."

The hot days passed and the discussion continued. Meanwhile, the noise of the birds increased. Finally, those who wanted to kill the birds won the argument. The next day, the people began to kill the birds. In a few days there were no birds left and the streets of the village were as quiet as a graveyard. The people were able to relax under the big trees in quiet. For a while, they were pleased with what they had done.

1 What was the advantage of the trees for the villagers?
2 What was the disadvantage?
3 What was the quarrel about?
4 '... supported the suggestion ...'. Find a word in the story which is the opposite in meaning to 'supported'.
5 'If we kill the birds, we will all have to pay the price one day.' This means
    A One day we will have to pay a lot of money to kill the birds,
    B One day we will suffer for killing the birds,
    C One day the birds will have to pay if we kill them.
6 '... the noise of the birds increased.' This means
    A the noise got louder,   B the noise got quieter,
    C the noise stayed the same.
7 '... the streets of the village were as quiet as a graveyard'. This means
    A it was not very quiet,   B everyone died,   C it was very quiet.
8 Did the villagers think they had done the right thing?

C Reading 2

Before reading: Do you think the villagers did the right thing? What do you think will happen?

After a time, the villagers began to be disturbed by small insects falling from the trees above them. They had insects in their eyes, ears, noses and mouths. It became worse and worse until they could not sit under the trees. Then they understood that the birds had eaten the insects. With no birds to eat them, the insects covered the whole village. Then they spread to the fields around the village and began to eat the crops.

Now the people saw how foolish they had been to kill the birds. The chief and elders met to decide what to do. They turned to the wise man who had spoken about nature. He told them there was no easy solution to their problem. They had to let nature repair the damage. So they decided no more birds should be killed and any birds passing by should be welcomed.

Over a long time, birds began to return. The villagers left them in peace and, little by little, the birds' song grew louder. As this happened, the number of insects decreased. Finally, the people could sit under the trees again.

The chief called a meeting and asked the people to learn their lesson. The villagers who had wanted to kill the birds lowered their heads in shame. They agreed that, in the future, everyone should respect the ways of nature and never kill creatures for no good reason.

D Comprehension 2

1 They 'began to be disturbed by small insects'. This means
   A the insects bit them,   B the insects troubled them,
   C they troubled the insects.
2 Why could the villagers no longer sit under the trees?
3 Why were there so many insects?
4 Why did they have another meeting?
5 What did they decide to do?
6 Find a word in the story which means 'get fewer in number'.
7 '… lowered their heads in shame.' This means
   A they felt happy,   B they felt sad,   C they felt guilty.
8 What is the lesson the chief wanted the people to learn?

Word focus

Make sentences with these words:

quarrel   shade   popular   unfortunately   increase   decrease
disturb   damage   shame   creature

E Grammar

1 Look.

Read these ways of describing things.

   *It was **as quiet as a graveyard**.*   *She ran **like a cheetah**.*

This kind of comparison is called a **simile**. It compares one thing to another using
as … as or **like …** . It can make your writing more interesting.

2 Complete these similes. Use the name of the most appropriate animal.

   bat   cheetah   bee   kitten   pig   lion   owl   ox

(a) as brave as a _____   (b) as fat as a _____
(c) as busy as a _____   (d) as strong as an _____
(e) as wise as an _____   (f) as blind as a _____
(g) as playful as a _____   (h) as fast as a _____

3 Make *three* more similes about animals.

bite like a crocodile

run like an antelope

4 Look.

> A **metaphor** also helps to make descriptions interesting. A metaphor doesn't compare two things; it says one thing **is** another.
>
> Simile: *He is **as brave as** a lion.*   Metaphor: *He **is** a lion.*
> Simile: *Ugo ran **like** a cheetah.*   Metaphor: *Ugo **is** a cheetah.*

5 Are these similes or metaphors?

   (a) She is a busy bee.   (b) She is as busy as a bee.
   (c) It was as dark as night.   (d) He ran like the wind.
   (e) He is a donkey.   (f) The storm is a howling monster.

6 Write a simile or metaphor for the following.

   (a) the sea   (b) the rain
   (c) the wind   (d) the moon
   (e) a favourite sportsman or woman

F Speech

1 Find *one* simile and *one* metaphor in this poem.
   Sleep *by* Pauline Stewart
   Sleep is a shy dancer
   who hides
   most of the day away.
   Sleep is sometimes heavy
   sometimes light
   like a blanket
   spread at night
   pressing down on tired bodies.

2 Recite the poem.

3 These pairs of words are sometimes confused. Say the words carefully.

   (a) quiet   quite   (b) chief   chef
   (c) wear   were   (d) walk   work
   (e) diary   dairy   (f) soap   soup
   (g) kitchen   chicken   (h) recipe   receipt

4 Write a sentence for each word. Read your sentences aloud.

G Dictation

Look at the words below. They are all in the dictation you are going to do. Then listen to your teacher and write the paragraph.

> conservation   protection   nature   environment   destroy   extinct

H Composition

1 Look.

In the story, 'The quarrel', there are some words that tell you about the time when something happened:

> *The hot days passed and the discussion continued.* **Meanwhile**, *the noise of the birds increased.*

Meanwhile means 'continuing at the same time'.

> *Finally, those who wanted to kill the birds won the argument.*

Finally means '*at the end*'.

2 Read the story again from 'The hot days passed …' and make a note of all the words you can find that tell you about the time something happened.

3 Compare your list with a partner.

4 Write *one* sentence for each time word or phrase you found.

(a) I wrote the answer to the question; <u>meanwhile</u> my friend did the same thing.

(b) <u>Finally</u>, we both got the correct answer.

(c) …

5 Write the story of 'The quarrel' from the point of view of one of the people in the village.

Imagine that you live in the village in the story. You can choose to be one of the following people:

- the village chief,
- the wise man who talked about nature,
- an ordinary person in the village.

Think about the following questions.

- What happened?
- What did you think about killing the birds?
- What did you say to other people about it?

Fun box

An old woman had two donkeys. Every morning she took them down the road to the fields.

One morning, the old woman was walking with her donkeys when she met two naughty boys. They shouted, "Good morning, mother of donkeys!"

The old woman smiled at them and said, "Good morning, my sons."

12 A pronunciation guide

A Reading

Before reading: What uses can you think of for a dictionary?

Dictionaries give help with pronunciation using **symbols**. These symbols are usually found between two lines / /. Look at the dictionary entry below and find the pronunciation symbols.

> **knee** /niː/ *noun* the part of your leg that bends: *He fell and cut his knee.*

To understand how you pronounce each symbol you have to find the **pronunciation guide** in your dictionary. It is usually at the very beginning or end. Find it now in your dictionary.

Here is the pronunciation guide from one dictionary:

Consonants								
p	pea	/piː/	f	fast	/faːst/	h	hot	/hɒt/
b	bee	/biː/	v	van	/væn/	m	man	/mæn/
t	tea	/tiː/	θ	thin	/θɪn/	n	no	/nəʊ/
d	day	/deɪ/	ð	this	/ðɪs/	ŋ	sing	/sɪŋ/
k	can	/kæn/	s	sit	/sɪt/	l	leg	/leg/
g	gap	/gæp/	z	zoo	/zuː/	r	red	/red/
tʃ	chip	/tʃɪp/	ʃ	shoe	/ʃuː/	j	yes	/jes/
dʒ	jar	/dʒaː/	ʒ	vision	/vɪʒn/	w	wet	/wet/
Vowels								
iː	see	/siː/	ɔː	saw	/sɔː/	əʊ	go	/gəʊ/
i	happy	/hæpi/	ʌ	cut	/cʌt/	aɪ	five	/faɪv/
ɪ	sit	/sɪt/	ʊ	book	/bʊk/	a	now	/naʊ/
e	bed	/bed/	uː	too	/tuː/	ɔɪ	boy	/bɔɪ/
æ	bad	/bæd/	ɔː	bird	/bɛːd/	ɪə	hear	/lɪə/
aː	father	/faːðə/	ə	about	/əbaʊt/	eə	hair	/heə/
ɒ	hot	/hɒt/	eɪ	say	/seɪ/	ʊə	pure	/pʊə/

B Comprehension

1 The pronunciation symbol for s is /s/. Write down the pronunciation symbols for the following letters.

(a) t   (b) v   (c) ch   (d) sh   (e) j

2 Match these words with their pronunciation symbols.

(a) lip   (i) /taɪm/
(b) lid   (ii) /lɪd/
(c) time   (iii) /taɪp/
(d) tide   (iv) /lɪp/
(e) type   (v) /taɪd/

3 Look at the pronunciation guide. Find out what these words are.

(a) /seɪ/   (b) /rɪŋ/   (c) /ʃiːp/   (d) /ʃəʊ/   (e) /ʃuːt/

4 Write the pronunciation symbols for the following words:

(a) pot   (b) bit   (c) me   (d) sad   (e) toy

Ⓒ Reading and comprehension 2

Follow the instructions and the diagrams to make a paper plane.

1 Take a piece of paper about
   30 cm by 21 cm.
2 Fold it down the centre and
   then open it out again.

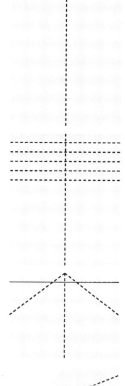

3 Fold down the top 2 cm.
4 Fold the top down again,
   and then 3 times more.
   You will have folded down
   almost half of the paper.

5 Now fold the top corners in to
   the centre line.
6 Fold along the centre line.

7 Fold down on both sides to
   make wings.

8 Your plane should look like this.

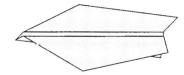

Now fly it!

D Grammar

1 Look.

An **antonym** has the opposite meaning to another word.
  start – stop   *open – close*   *increase – decrease*
A **synonym** has a similar meaning to another word.
  start – begin   *shut – close*   *mend – repair*
Antonyms and synonyms are tested in the Common Entrance exam.

2 Write an antonym for each of these words.
  (a) remember   (b) late   (c) take
  (d) always   (e) pleasant   (f) warm
  (g) rich   (h) narrow   (i) ill

3 Write a synonym for each of these words.
  (a) discover   (b) rich   (c) happy
  (d) quickly   (e) pleasant   (f) wonderful
  (g) exhausted   (h) impolite   (i) enormous

4 Choose sentences from the box to complete the dialogues.

We often use antonyms when we reply to what someone says.
  *I don't want to be **late** to school.*   *I agree, it's better to be **early**.*

It could be more positive.   No, it's quite cool.
No, I had a terrible day!   Good, you don't want to forget that.
Well, he's not poor!

  (a) I've remembered where I put my money. ...
  (b) Is he rich? ...
  (c) This school report is very negative, isn't it? ...
  (d) Did you have a pleasant day? ...
  (e) It's not very warm in here, is it? ...

5 Practise the dialogues. Work in pairs.

6 Rewrite the sentences. Replace the underlined word with a synonym.
  (a) We were very <u>glad</u> to see him.
  (b) Are you <u>certain</u> you can't find your dictionary?
  (c) My mother gave me my birthday <u>present</u> yesterday.
  (d) I was surprised to <u>receive</u> it before my birthday.
  (e) He was <u>tired</u> after running the 400 metres race.
  (f) I'm <u>frightened</u> of snakes.

E Speech

1 The pairs of words in column A have one sound the same. Use the pronunciation guide in your dictionary (or the one on page 54) to find the symbol for the sound and write it in column B.

A	B
pit – sat	/t/
true – shoe	/u:/
bit – bead	_____
read – wrote	_____
way – what	_____
she – fish	_____
thin – thief	_____
then – those	_____
boot – rude	_____
church – beach	_____
yes – young	_____
key – sick	_____

2 Find words from the box that rhyme with the words below.

> again   five   by   shout   shirt   short   gate   saw   feet

(a) about _____   (b) sigh _____   (c) ought _____
(d) alive _____   (e) hurt _____   (f) train _____
(g) wait _____   (h) neat _____   (i) or _____

3 Find the word which does not rhyme with the others.
(a) snake   lake   sack   cake
(b) lost   most   roast   post
(c) three   see   we   tie
(d) show   grew   blue   do
(e) eight   hate   late   about

F Dictation

Look at the words below. They are all in the dictation you are going to do. Then listen to your teacher and write the paragraph.

> reference   information   dictionary   thesaurus   synonym

G Composition

1 You are going to write a composition about 'Transport in Nigeria'.

In this type of composition you have to explain something. You must just give facts and information. You do not give your opinions.
- Give the facts in a clear order.
- Make one point clearly in each paragraph.
- Make the point in the first sentence of the paragraph.
- Then add one or two sentences to give examples.

Put these sentences in the best order.
(a) They are cheaper than most other forms of transport.
(b) Buses run all over the country.
(c) One popular means of transport is the bus.

2 Write similar paragraphs on
(a) trains,   (b) planes.

3 Complete this opening paragraph.

In the opening paragraph state what you are going to write about in the composition.

There are many means of transport used in Nigeria. For example, ...

4 Complete this closing paragraph.

Your closing paragraph should sum up what you have said and make it clear that you have finished.

In conclusion, we can say that Nigeria has many means of transport. The most popular is ...   The most expensive is ...

5 Write your paragraphs in the correct order and complete the composition.

You can use some of these link words.
For example, ...   In addition, ...   Moreover, ...   Finally, ...   In conclusion, ...

Fun box

Did you know ...

... **Sure** and **sugar** are the only two words in English which are spelt 'su' but pronounced 'sh'?

... only two words in the English language end in the letters 'gry' – they are **angry** and **hungry**?

13 Safe water

A Reading 1

Before reading: Make a list all the things you have used water for today.

Water is very important for life. All humans, animals and plants need water to live and to grow. We can all live for a week, even a month, without food but we cannot live for more than a few days without water.

Water is everywhere around us. It is at home, school and in hospitals. When it rains it drips from plants, umbrellas, rooftops and makes puddles on the roads. We use water in our homes for drinking, bathing, cooking and washing. We use water to wash cars and to water our gardens. Farmers need water for their crops and for their animals. In factories we use water for many things, for example to cool hot metals. We also use it to produce electricity, for example from the hydroelectric works at Kanji dam.

We all need fresh, safe, unsalted water to drink. The water we use comes from rivers and lakes. We do not usually use sea water because it is salty. Salt can be taken out of sea water in a process called **desalination** but it is very expensive.

We call the water in lakes and rivers **fresh water** but that does not mean it is safe to drink. It can contain sand, dirt and oil. It also contains living things (called **bacteria**) that can cause serious diseases like cholera and dysentery. Before water is safe for us to drink, it has to be treated.

B Comprehension 1

1 How long can humans live without water?
2 Make lists of the uses of water in the text under *three* headings.
   (a) at home   (b) at work   (c) other uses
3 Think of *five* more uses of water. Add these to your lists.
4 The process of desalination is the process of
   A putting salt in water,   B taking salt out of water,
   C making water very expensive.
5 What causes cholera and dysentery?
6 Is fresh water from a river safe to drink?

59

Before reading: How can water be treated to make it safe?

In cities, water is pumped out of the rivers and lakes and treated. It is passed through a filter to take out the dirt. Afterwards, the bacteria in the water is killed by bubbling chlorine gas through it. Then the clean water is pumped down pipes to where we need it for drinking, cooking, flushing toilets and bathing.

If the water you use in your home is not treated, you must treat it yourself. The most important thing to do is to boil the water. This kills the bacteria. The water can then be filtered to clean out the dirt.

Experiment to filter dirty water

You need:
- a large plastic bottle with the bottom cut off
- an empty container
- small stones
- gravel (very small stones)
- sand
- muddy, dirty water

dirty water

sand

gravel

small stones

plastic bottle

clean water

1 Wash the stones, gravel and sand.
2 Turn the bottle upside down and fill as shown in the diagram.
3 Pour in the dirty water.
4 Collect the clear water that comes out of the bottom.

Be careful! The water may be clear now, but it might still contain bacteria. Do ***not*** drink it.

Sometimes, we take water for granted. We turn on a tap at home or school and out gushes safe, clean water. However, water is precious. If we waste water now, we will not have it in the future. Water will become scarcer as there are more people in the world. We have to be more careful or there will not be enough for everyone. Everybody should use water more wisely. We must all help to save water in our homes, at school and everywhere.

D Comprehension 2

1 What does a filter do?
2 What is used to kill bacteria?
3 If the water in your home is untreated, what is the most important thing to do?
4 What is the purpose of the experiment?
5 Look at the experiment.
   Why should you not drink the filtered water?
6 '... we take water for granted.' This means
   A we don't think seriously about water,
   B we don't pay for water,
   C we waste water.
7 'Water will become scarcer ...'. This means
   A there will be more water,
   B the water will be dirtier,
   C there will be less water.
8 How do you think we can save water?
   Make a list of your ideas.

Word focus

Make sentences with these words:

human   drip   puddle   factory   filter   flush   gravel   granted
gush   scarce

E Grammar

1 Complete the sentences with **some** or **any**.

Some means 'part' or 'not all'. **Any** means 'all' or 'none'.

I like
some *fruit*

I don't like
some *fruit*

I like
any *fruit*

I don't like
any *fruit*

(a) I love _____ kind of vegetable. There's nothing I don't like.
(b) I like _____ fruit, but not all.
(c) I don't like _____ insects. They frighten me.
(d) You can catch _____ bus to the hospital. They all go there.
(e) _____ of the buses go to the market, but _____ don't.

2 Complete the sentences with **some** or **any**.

> **Some** is most often used in positive sentences and **any** is most often used in questions and negatives.
>
> *Have you got **any** money?   No, I don't have **any**./Yes, I have **some**.*

(a) Have you got _____ brothers or sisters?

(b) There are _____ books on the desk.

(c) Do we have _____ sugar?

(d) No, we don't have _____ sugar.

(e) I'll buy _____ sugar.

3 Complete the sentences. Use the words in the box.

> With **some, any, no** and **every**, we use
> + **where** for places
> + **thing** for objects or animals
> + **body** or + **one** for people
>
> *I've seen you **somewhere** before.   I've looked **everywhere** for her.*
> *There's **nothing** in this desk.   We didn't catch **anything** in the hunt.*
> *Is there **anybody** there?   No, there isn't **anyone** outside.*

> somewhere   everything   anywhere   everywhere   everywhere
> anybody   something   nowhere

(a) Can you come here? I want to tell you _____ .

(b) My father knows _____ about computers.

(c) Has _____ seen my pen?

(d) I've lost my pen. I've looked _____ but I can't find it _____ .

(e) The rain is very heavy! Let's find _____ to shelter.

(f) There is _____ to shelter. I've looked _____ .

F Speech

1 Practise the questions with falling intonation.

> With **Wh- questions**, we usually use falling intonation at the end.
>
> *What are we going to do?*

(a) What equipment do we need?

(b) Where can we get some dirty water?

(c) What do we have to do?

(d) Where does the water come out?

(e) How do we collect the water?

(f) What does that show us?

2 Practise the dialogues in pairs. Use falling and rising intonation.

When we use a **Wh- question** to ask someone to repeat information, or to show surprise at the answer, we use rising intonation.	**A:** *Where are you from?*↗ **B:** *China.* **A:** *Where?*↗

(a) *A:* What's your name?
    B: George Bush.
    A: What?

(b) *A:* What are we going to do?
    B: Filter some dirty water.
    A: Why?

(c) *A:* Where does the water come out?
    B: From the top of the bottle.
    A: From where?

3 Talk about the experiment to filter water. Work in pairs.

- A asks the questions in 1 on page 62. If you need to ask B to repeat anything, use rising intonation.

- B looks at the details of the experiment on page 60.

G Dictation

Look at the words below. They are all in the dictation you are going to do. Then listen to your teacher and write the paragraph.

scientist	observe	explain	experiment	test	idea	discover

H Composition

1 Copy and complete this record of the experiment to filter dirty water.

<u>Experiment:</u>	to filter dirty water
<u>Equipment used:</u>	1 a large 2 an empty 3 ...
<u>Procedure:</u>	1 We washed the ... 2 The bottle was turned upside down and ... 3 ...
<u>Results:</u>	(put these words in the correct order): out filtered The water sand and gravel stones dirt the of the The stones, gravel and

2 Write about an experiment you did in a science lesson.

When you write about an experiment, you have to write what you did or observed. Give the facts in order. Don't give opinions.

14 The oceans

A Reading 1

Before reading: What do you think a marine biologist does?

The children's teacher has invited a visitor to come to speak to the class.

Marine biologist

Teacher: We're very lucky today that Dr Grace Orji has come to visit us. She's a marine biologist and she's going to tell us about her work. Then she'll answer your questions.

Dr Orji: Good morning, children. First of all, let me tell you what a marine biologist does. I am a scientist, but a special kind of scientist, a biologist. Does anyone know what biology is?

Ugo: It's something to do with animals and plants.

Dr Orji: Exactly. Biology is the study of living things. A biologist is someone who studies living things. Animals and plants are living things but I don't study them because I'm a *marine* biologist. Can anyone tell us what 'marine' means?

Sakiru: Is it something to do with ships?

Dr Orji: Yes, it is. Ships sail on the sea and 'marine' means something to do with the sea. But a marine biologist studies living things in the sea. I study the fish in the ocean off the coast of Nigeria. Today I'll answer any questions that you have about the oceans, seas and the life in them. So put up your hands and ask your questions.

Zarat: What is the difference between an ocean and a sea?

Dr Orji: Oceans are very big. There are four huge areas of water that we call oceans – the Pacific, the Atlantic, the Indian and the Arctic oceans. Seas are smaller areas of water.

Tunde: What do we use the seas and oceans for?

Dr Orji: The main uses are for transport and for fishing. Ships and boats are very important forms of transport on seas, lakes and rivers. Seas and oceans also give us an important source of food – fish.

B Comprehension 1

1 Why is Dr Orji in the classroom?
2 What is 'biology'?
3 What does 'marine' mean?
4 What does a marine biologist do?
5 How many oceans are there?
6 What are the two main uses of the oceans and seas?

C Reading 2

Before reading: What questions would you like to ask Dr Orji about fish?

Adanmi: How many different types of fish are there?

Dr Orji: We know of about twenty thousand different types but there may be many more. Fish can live very deep in the oceans where it's difficult to study them. We know there are fish living at more than ten kilometres below the surface of the sea, but we don't know how many types there are down there.

Hauwa: How do fish breathe in the water?

Dr Orji: Fish have entrances on the sides of their bodies called gills. As the water passes over the gills, oxygen is taken out of the water and into the body of the fish. Here's a picture of a fish which shows its gills.

Ahmed: How do fish swim?

Dr Orji: By flapping their tails from side to side, sometimes very fast. Tuna and some sharks can swim at eighty kilometres per hour.

Yemi: Do fish sleep?

Dr Orji: That's difficult to answer. They don't have eyelids so they can't close their eyes, but most do rest. Sometimes they just float or sometimes they find a place to lie. Their eyes are always open, though, and they look out for danger.

Ugo: Which is the biggest fish?

Dr Orji: The biggest is the whale shark which can be seventeen metres long. And the smallest is the goby which is only about one centimetre long.

Tunde: Which is the most dangerous fish?

Dr Orji: The shark, of course. Most sharks don't attack people, but some will. The great white shark is the most dangerous. I have a picture of one here.

gills   scales

fins

D Comprehension 2

Match the questions with their answers.

1 Which is the most dangerous fish?

2 How many different types of fish are there?

3 How do fish swim?

4 Which is the biggest fish?

5 Do fish sleep?

6 How do fish breathe?

(a) Over twenty thousand different types are known but there may be more.

(b) As water passes over their gills, oxygen is taken into their bodies.

(c) The whale shark – it's over 17 metres long.

(d) They can't close their eyes but they do rest.

(e) The great white shark.

(f) By flapping their tails from side to side.

Word focus 🔍

Make sentences with these words:

biology   marine   surface   flap   eyelid   float   whale   shark

E Grammar

1 Make *ten* words using one word from box A and one word from box B.

(a) seashell

A
sea   bed   foot   butter
time   air   grand   book
sun   ear

B
glasses   table   room
ring   shell   ball   mother
case   port   fly

2 Complete the sentences with compound nouns from the box.

Nouns made up of two small words are called **compound nouns**.

Some compound nouns are written as one word – *bathroom*.
Many are written as two words – *marine biologist, whale shark*.
A few are written with a hyphen – *dining-room*.

alarm clock   toothbrush   traffic jam   waiting room   traffic lights
post office

(a) The _____ aren't working. They stay on the red light all the time.

(b) I'm going to the _____ to buy some stamps.

(c) I can't clean my teeth because I've lost my _____.

(d) I didn't wake up this morning because I didn't hear my _____.

(e) It took an hour to drive to school today. We were stuck in a _____.

(f) The nurse told us to wait in the hospital _____.

66

3 Write *one* sentence for each of the compound nouns to show their meaning. (You can use a dictionary to help you.)
   (a) passenger seat   (b) ticket office   (c) ashtray
   (d) toothpaste   (e) door handle   (f) phone card

F Speech

1 Read aloud your sentences in Grammar 2 and 3. Make sure you pronounce the compound nouns with the correct stress.

> In compound nouns, the first word has the main stress. This stress is often shown in dictionaries with this mark: '.
>
> 'bathroom   mar'ine bi'ologist   a'larm clock

2 Ask and answer the questions in Comprehension 2 on page 66.

G Dictation

Look at the words below. They are all in the dictation you are going to do. Then listen to your teacher and write the paragraph.

> ocean   transport   canoe   sailing ship   nowadays   navy   war

H Composition

1 Write *two* paragraphs about fish. Use the text and the notes below.
   Paragraph 1: where fish live; how they breathe; how fish swim
   Paragraph 2: how many types of fish there are;
                  the biggest and smallest fish; the most dangerous fish

2 Write *three* paragraphs about the oceans and seas. The first sentence of each paragraph is given.
   Paragraph 1: There are many seas and four oceans in the world.
   Paragraph 2: Oceans, seas, lakes and rivers are used for transport.
   Paragraph 3: The other main use of the oceans and seas is as a source of food.

Fun box

Did you know ...

- ... some fish can swim backwards?   • ... some fish live for up to fifty years?
- ... in Japan, they eat a lot of raw (uncooked) fish? Perhaps that is why there are more very old people in Japan than in any other country. A fisherman from Japan, Shigechio Isumi, was 120 when he died.
- ... a blue whale weighs as much as 1900 men?

15 Health and drugs

A Reading 1

Before reading: What are 'human internal organs'? Can you name any?

The human body is like a machine. It is made up of thousands of parts all of which work together. Our bones make a skeleton that contains all the other parts. The working parts of the body are called **organs**. Two of the most important organs are the brain and the heart.

The brain is like a computer. It receives information and uses it. Our ears, eyes, tongue, nose and hands all provide plenty of information for the brain. It thinks about the information and then sends messages to the other parts of the body to make us act.

The heart is a pump, sending blood around the body to reach all parts.

Like machines, we have to take good care of our bodies. If we don't give a machine oil and fuel it will stop working. In the same way, if we don't drink, eat good food and sleep well, our bodies will break down. We will become ill.

The brain tells the body what to do

The heart pumps blood around the body

The skeleton is the frame of the body

When we are healthy our bodies can fight diseases and germs, but sometimes things can go wrong. Then we might need medicines to help repair our bodies.

B Comprehension 1

1 Find two similes in the text.
2 What is a skeleton made of?
3 What sends information to the brain?
4 What does the brain do with the information?
5 What does a heart do?
6 What happens when a machine is not looked after?
7 What happens when our bodies are not looked after?
8 Why might we need to take medicines?

C Reading 2

Before reading: What are the advantages of drugs? What are the disadvantages?

We use medical drugs to treat illnesses. We get them when the doctor writes a prescription, or we can buy them at the pharmacy.

Sometimes we use drugs to prevent illness. Doctors and nurses give us drugs called vaccines. These drugs stop people from getting serious diseases such as whooping cough, measles and polio.

All drugs have an effect on our bodies. Most help us. However, we always have to be careful when using drugs.

There are many risks when taking drugs. You should only use drugs that the doctor prescribes, and you should only take the amount of the drug that the doctor tells you to take. If people use the same drugs for a long time, it can have a bad effect. Drugs can cause changes to the body or the brain. Some drugs act on the brain and change the way we feel, think or act, making us feel worried or sad.

There are some drugs which are natural. For example, cigarettes are made of tobacco leaves from the tobacco plant. Wine, which some adults drink, is made from grapes. These contain some drugs which can also be dangerous. You should not touch them until you are an adult.

All countries, like Nigeria, have laws for drugs. In most countries, drugs like caffeine found in coffee, alcohol found in beer and wine, and nicotine in cigarettes are OK for adults to take. However, all countries ban dangerous drugs.

D Comprehension 2

1 How can we get medical drugs?
2 '... we use medical drugs to treat illness'. This means
   A the drugs make the illness better,
   B the drugs stop us getting the illness,
   C the drugs give us the illness.
3 What are the drugs that prevent illness called?
4 What are measles, whooping cough and polio?
5 What can happen if we take drugs for too long?
6 Name two natural products which contain drugs.
7 What is nicotine?
8 '... all countries ban dangerous drugs.' This means
   A all countries have dangerous drugs,
   B all countries use dangerous drugs,
   C all countries stop dangerous drugs.

E Grammar

1 Look.

A **prefix** is a group of letters that goes at the beginning of a word. The letters change its meaning.

Prefix	Meaning	Examples
un-	not	unchanged, untouched
dis-	opposite	disagree, dislike
re-	again	refill, rewrite
over-	too much	overdo, oversleep
under-	not enough	underused, undercooked

2 Use the prefixes in the table above to make new words from the words in the box below. Write them in columns as below. Some words can take more than one prefix.

likely   sure   eat   comfortable   honest   usual   tired   appear
crowded   make   weight   obey   common   populated   do

un-	dis-	re-	over-	under-
unlikely				

3 Think of *three* more words using one of these prefixes.
4 Write *six* sentences to show the use of six of the words with prefixes.
5 Look.

A **suffix** is a group of letters that goes at the end of a word. The letters make a new word. You know the first two kinds of suffixes.

* **-ing** and **-ed** are used with verbs: *walk/walking/walked*
* **-er** and **-est** are used with adjectives: *fast/faster/fastest*
* **-ly** changes adjectives to adverbs: *quick/quickly, shy/shyly*
* **-ness** and **-ity** change adjectives to nouns: *sick/sickness, stupid/stupidity*

6 Use the suffixes **-ity** or **-ness** to write the nouns in the table.

7 Write *six* sentences to show the use of the nouns.

Adjective	Noun	Adjective	Noun
stupid		sad	
similar		weak	
popular		dark	

70

F Speech

1 These words all have prefixes. Say them with your teacher and then write them in the correct column. Put in the stress mark.

> impolite   dissatisfied   impossible   unreliable   dishonest   informal
> inexpensive   incorrect   unacceptable

• ' ● •	• • ' ●	• • ' ● •	• ' ● • •
			im'possible

2 Say the words.

> The addition of some suffixes can change the pronunciation.
> * **-ity** moves the stress: 'stupid → stu'pidity
> * **-ion** (added to a verb to make a noun): 'educate → edu'cation

(a) 'similar/simi'larity   (b) 'popular/popu'larity   (c) e'lect/e'lection

(d) 'punctual/punctu'ality   (e) dis'cuss/dis'cussion   (f) 'hesitate/hesi'tation

3 Say these sentences.

(a) Their opinions in the discussion were very similar.

(b) He is very popular so I'm sure he'll win the election.

(c) If you want to be punctual, you must show no hesitation.

G Dictation

Look at the words below. They are all in the dictation you are going to do. Then listen to your teacher and write the paragraph.

> drugs   illegal   user   banned   arrest   addictive   addict

H Composition

1 Write *two* paragraphs about medical drugs. Use the information from the text and the notes below.

Paragraph 1: the normal use of drugs; why we take them; how we get them; how we should use them

Paragraph 2: the misuse of drugs; what happens if we use drugs for too long; what happens if we use the wrong drugs; what drugs we shouldn't take

2 Write a short conversation between two friends, A and B.

* A wants to smoke a cigarette and drink some beer.
* B explains the dangers and persuades A not to do it.

16 Finding out about HIV/AIDS

A Reading 1

Before reading: What illnesses and diseases can you name?

When Aliu heard about HIV and AIDS on the radio, he didn't know what they were. He knew about cholera and malaria, and he had had coughs and colds. He decided to ask Ugo about HIV and AIDS the next day at school.

At break, he found Ugo. "Ugo, can I ask you a question?"

"Of course," she answered. "What's the question?"

"What are HIV and AIDS?"

Ugo looked serious and said, "I know a bit about both but not a lot. I know that HIV turns to AIDS and AIDS has no cure."

Aliu was disappointed because he had thought she could tell him all about both.

"We could find out more in the library you know," she smiled.

"Really?" His face lit up.

"Yes, let's go!" He followed her shyly into the library.

Aliu didn't often go into the library. He preferred to play outside. However, Ugo loved reading. Sometimes, she read storybooks and information books.

Inside the library, Ugo knew what to do. She looked at the books arranged neatly on one of the shelves. She picked one up.

"Here," she whispered, "this should tell us something about HIV and AIDS."

They sat down, opened the book and read the contents page. It had a lot of chapters on HIV and AIDS.

B Comprehension 1

1 How did Aliu hear about HIV and AIDS?
2 How did he decide to find out what they were?
3 How much did Ugo know about them?
4 What did she know?
5 How did they decide to find out more?
6 Why do you think Aliu 'followed her shyly into the library'?
7 Which page did they look at first in the book?
8 What was the book about?

C Reading 2

Before reading: What do you know about HIV and AIDS?

"First of all, what's HIV?" asked Aliu.

"Let's see," said Ugo.

She turned to the back of the book and found the index. She read the entry 'HIV 24', so she turned to page 24 of the book. There she found a section about HIV.

She read what she found to Aliu, "HIV is short for 'Human Immunodeficiency Virus'."

Aliu looked surprised, "They're difficult words."

"Yes," answered Ugo. "And it says AIDS is short for 'Acquired Immune Deficiency Syndrome'. The letters that start each word have been put together to make new, simple words, AIDS and HIV."

"Oh, I see, but what do they mean?" asked Aliu.

"Let's read this and find out," said Ugo.

They read quietly for five minutes and learnt some important facts. They found out that HIV lives in the blood. It only passes from one person to another through body fluids, usually blood. This can happen when people have accidents, or have injections with dirty needles.

In the next part of the book they read that HIV will change to AIDS one day. However, there are now some drugs that make this take longer. When someone gets AIDS they will get ill, and then die.

The children thought that was very sad but then they read that it is not easy to get HIV. You cannot get it by talking to people, touching them, or even kissing them. People who have HIV are not ill and can live normal lives.

They also learnt that people can protect themselves from getting HIV. It is important not to use a needle for an injection that has been used by someone else. It is also important to take care in accidents where there is blood around.

D Comprehension 2

1 What part of the book did Ugo look at to find the correct page?
2 Where was the index in the book?
3 On what page did they find the information they wanted?
4 If Acquired Immune Deficiency Syndrome is called AIDS for short, what are these called for short?
   (a) Nigerian Broadcasting Corporation   (b) United Nations
   (c) United States of America   (d) West African Exams Council

5 Are these statements true or false?

    (a) HIV lives in the blood.

    (b) Dirty needles can pass HIV from one person to another.

    (c) It is easy to catch HIV/AIDS.

    (d) You can catch HIV/AIDS from someone by touching them.

    (e) You can catch HIV/AIDS from someone if their blood gets into your body.

    (f) People with AIDS can get better.

    (g) People are not ill when they have HIV.

    (h) People are not ill when they have AIDS.

Word focus

Make sentences with these words:

cure   contents page   chapter   index   entry   section   fluid   protect

E Grammar

1 Look.

These **suffixes** can be used to make an adjective from a noun or verb:

-ous *fame/famous*	**-ive** *create/creative*
-al *music/musical*	**-able** *enjoy/enjoyable*
-y *dirt/dirty*	

The suffix **-ful** means 'full of': *thought/thoughtful, help/helpful*
The suffix **-less** means 'without': *thought/thoughtless, help/helpless*

2 Make adjectives from the nouns in the box.

danger   politics   cloud   attract   drink   pain   job   fog   fame
comfort   use   break

3 Make *ten* sentences to show the use of the adjectives.

4 Look.

Word families are groups of words that are related in meaning to each other. Some of them use a prefix or a suffix.

    If you know the meaning of one, you can usually work out the meaning of others in the same word family.

    enter – entry – entrance   *electricity – electric – electrification*

5 Find and write the words from the same word families.

> treat   prefer   simple   unopened   untreated   opening   uninformed
> preferred   protection   oversimplify   open   information   preference
> simplification   protect   treatment   inform   unprotected

6 Write *six* sentences to show the meaning of *six* words which are new to you from the box in 5.

F Speech

1 Say the words.

Different members of a word family can have word stress in different postions.

Verb	Noun
pre'fer	'preference
in'form	infor'mation
ex'plain	expla'nation
in'ject	in'jection
'multiply	multipli'cation
'operate	ope'ration

Verb	Noun
'simple	simplifi'cation
'stupid	stu'pidity
'generous	gene'rosity
'active	'action
e'lectric	elec'tricity
cou'rageous	'courage

2 Write *five* sentences using words from above. Read your sentences aloud.

3 Make a wall poster in a group. The aim is to inform people of an important health message. Choose something you think is important to do with HIV/AIDS or drug abuse. Discuss with your teacher and your group what you want to say about the topic. Look back at the texts on pages 72 and 73 for information.

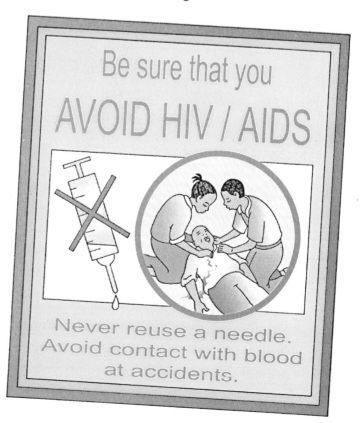

Be sure that you AVOID HIV / AIDS

Never reuse a needle. Avoid contact with blood at accidents.

G Dictation

Look at the words below. They are all in the dictation you are going to do.
Then listen to your teacher and write the paragraph.

> HIV/AIDS   problem   1980s   originally   virus   human   millions   disease

H Composition

1 Write a letter to tell a friend about the poster you made in Speech on page 75. Explain what you did and what lesson you wanted to teach about drugs or HIV/AIDS.

2 Look at the pictures and write a short report of what happened.

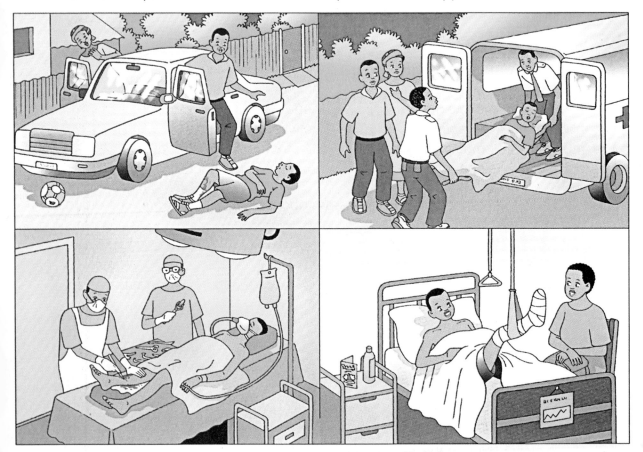

Fun box

Did you know ...

... in Germany people used to believe that kissing a donkey could stop toothache?

... a sneeze leaves your body at 65 kilometres per hour?

... in a normal life, a person's heart beats 2 000 000 000 times?

17 The stonecutter

A Reading 1

Before reading: Look at the picture. What is happening? What do you think the story is about?

There was once a poor, lonely stonecutter. He lived in a small hut with little food and few friends. One day, as he was busy working with his hammer and chisel on a huge rock, he heard the shouts of many people. He went out to see what was happening and found that the king was making a visit to the village. The stonecutter pushed his way to the front of the crowd and stared in amazement at the rich colours and gold thread of the king's clothes.

"I wish I were the king," he said to himself. "There is no one more powerful than a king."

His wish was heard and immediately the stonecutter became a powerful king. He found himself dressed in the finest clothes, riding a white horse and waving at the crowds of people who had come to see him.

"This is power," he said.

However, the new king was not happy for long. It was a hot, long dry season and everything began to suffer. The men and animals were weak and the crops died in the fields. The stonecutter king looked at the sky and realised that there were things more powerful than men.

He said to himself, "I wish I were as powerful as the sun, and then I would be happy."

Once again, his wish was granted immediately. The stonecutter enjoyed being the sun. Now he looked down on all the kingdoms of the earth, not just one. When he sent down his bright rays, he saw the kings and chiefs hide under their parasols. The ordinary men took shelter under the trees. He had the power to make the crops grow or die.

1 What tools did the stonecutter use?

2 What was the stonecutter doing when the king visited the village?

3 'The stonecutter … stared in amazement …' .This means
   A he was afraid of what he saw,
   B he was surprised at what he saw,
   C he wanted what he saw.

4 Was the stonecutter pleased when he became a king?

5 What happened to make him change his mind?

6 What did he want to become?

7 '…his wish was granted immediately.' This means
   A he got what he wanted,
   B he didn't get what he wanted,
   C he enjoyed being the sun.

8 Was he happy to be the sun?

C Reading 2

Before reading: Can you think of anything more powerful than the sun? What do you think will happen next in the story?

Then, one day, a small cloud drifted across the sky. It cut off the sun's rays. The stonecutter realised that there was something even more powerful than the sun.

"It's a pity I'm not a cloud," he said. "Then I would be really happy."

Again, his wish came true. He floated across the sky and blocked out the sun's rays. He felt very powerful and important. He grew stronger and became a huge rain cloud. When he burst open, he poured his waters down on the earth. There was a terrible flood and the roads and paths became rivers. Everything and everybody was washed out of his way; everything except for a huge rock that did not move.

"There is nothing as powerful as a rock," said the stonecutter. "How I wish I were a rock. Then I would be happy."

Of course, his wish came true once again. And, once again, he was happy for a time. He liked being a rock because he was untouched by sun or rain. He felt stronger than anything else in the whole of nature.

Then, one day, a man approached him, carrying a bag. The man opened his bag, took out a hammer and chisel and began to cut away at the rock.

"Oh! Now, finally, I understand," he said. "I wish I were a stonecutter again. Then I would be happy."

His wish came true. He became a stonecutter again. Once again, he lived in a small hut with little food and few friends and made his living with a hammer and chisel. However, this time he was happy.

D Comprehension 2

1 '... a small cloud drifted across the sky.' This means
   A the cloud stopped moving,
   B the cloud moved slowly,
   C the cloud moved quickly.
2 What did he think was more powerful than the sun?
3 He 'blocked out the sun's rays.' This means
   A he made the sun shine more strongly,
   B he made the sun shine less strongly,
   C he stopped the sun shining.
4 How did the cloud make a terrible flood?
5 What did he see that was more powerful than the floodwater?
6 Why did he like being a rock?
7 Why did he decide he wanted to be a stonecutter again?
8 What is the lesson of this story?

> **Word focus** 🔍 Make sentences with these words:
> amazement   rays   parasol   drift   block out   burst open

E Grammar

1 Look.

When we make a wish we often use **were**, not **was**.
   *I wish I **were** the king.*   *I wish I **were** rich.*
We also do this when we describe the result.
   *If I **were** rich, I would ('d) buy ice cream for all my friends every day.*

79

2 (a) Imagine you can have *three* wishes for yourself. Write your wishes.

   I wish I were taller.

   (b) Now write a sentence for each wish to describe the result.

   If I were taller, I'd be in the basketball team.

   (c) Read your sentences to some friends. Listen to their sentences.

3 Write *five* wishes for you and your family.

   I wish my father had a car. I wish my grandmother wasn't ill.

4 Make *five* sentences from the table.

If I were a	king, stonecutter, magician, teacher, famous singer,	I'd ...

F Speech

1 Look.

When we speak,
   we speak to someone – the **audience**
   for a reason – the **purpose**
   we choose the way of speaking – the **style**.
Imagine you want a sweet.
   Purpose: to ask for a sweet
   Audience: a friend who has a sweet
   Style: friendly, informal
   You say, *"Can I have a sweet, please?"*
Imagine you have to give a letter from your parents to the school principal.
   Purpose: to give the letter
   Audience: the school principal
   Style: polite, formal
   You say, *"May I give you this letter, please, Ma?"*

2 What would you say in these situations?

   (a) You want to invite a friend to your home.

   (b) You want to ask a teacher for permission to leave the classroom.

   (c) You want to ask your mother for some money.

   (d) You want to ask a shopkeeper for some soap.

   (e) You want to tell a doctor that you have a fever and a headache.

3 Act out the situations with a friend.

G Dictation

Look at the words below. They are all in the dictation you are going to do. Then listen to your teacher and write the paragraph.

> appropriate   level   formality   lack of   respect   inappropriate

H Composition

1 Look.

> We also have an **audience**, a **style** and a **purpose** when we write.

2 What are the purpose and audience for each of the texts below?

(a)
Dear Obi

Hi! How are you? It's my birthday next week and I'm having a party. Can you come?

(b)
Again, his wish came true. He floated across the sky and blocked out the sun's rays. He felt very powerful and important. He grew stronger and became a huge rain cloud. When he burst open, he poured his waters down on the earth.

(c) Open the box carefully.
   (i) Take out all the parts carefully and spread them out on a table.
   (ii) Check you have everything you need.
   (iii) Lay the back (part C) flat on the floor.

(d)
My shopping list
new pencils
a notebook
coffee and sugar (for Mum)

3 Imagine you want to visit another city in the next holiday. Your uncle, aunt and cousins live there. Write *two* short letters – think carefully about the **audience**, **purpose** and **style** for each.

   (a) A letter to a cousin who is the same age as you and you know very well. Tell your cousin that you want to visit.

   (b) A letter to your uncle to request permission to visit the family.

Fun box

Did you know ...

... in Ecuador, a country in South America, nearly 80 per cent of the people have been bitten by a snake?

... some of the world's most dangerous snakes live at the bottom of the sea?

... sometimes snakes are born with two heads – they fight each other for food?

18 Writing a story

A Reading 1

Before reading: What is your favourite story?

You know many stories. You have heard and read many stories at school and you may have heard even more at home, perhaps in a different language. You have also discussed stories in groups and even made up some of your own.

Now is the time to start using your experience to write better stories. Firstly, never forget that every story must have a beginning, a middle and an end. Also, all stories must have other things. They need to have a **setting**, **characters** and a **plot**.

Setting: This is **where** the story happens. The setting for 'The quarrel' (Module 11) is in a village.

Characters: This is **who** is in the story. The characters in 'The fire on the hill' (Module 4) are the judge, headman, rich merchant and young man.

Plot: This is **what** happens in the story. The plot of 'The stonecutter' (Module 17) is:

- A stonecutter saw the king and wished he was a king.
- He became a king. However, it was very hot and dry so everything in the kingdom suffered. He realised that the sun was more powerful than a king. He wished he was the sun.
- He became the sun. One day, a cloud blocked out the sun's rays. He realised a cloud was more powerful than the sun. He wished he was a cloud.
- He became a cloud. He became a rain cloud and sent down his waters to make a flood. Everything was washed out of the way except for a rock. He realised a rock was more powerful than a cloud or water. He wished he was a rock.
- He became a rock. One day, a stonecutter came and started cutting pieces off the rock. He realised a stonecutter was more powerful than a rock. He wished he was a stonecutter again.
- He became a stonecutter again. He was happy. He had learnt to be satisfied with what he was. He knew everyone and everything has its part to play in life.

B Comprehension 1

1 What is the setting for the story 'The fire on the hill' (Module 4)?
2 Think about a story called 'Saved!' Think of a setting for your story. It could be on a canoe, in the forest, in a cave, or even on a football field!
3 Who are the characters in 'The quarrel' (Module 11)?
4 Think about *three* characters you could have in your story, 'Saved!' Write their names.
5 Write a sentence about each to describe what they look like (tall, thin, ugly, etc.).
6 Write a sentence about each to describe what sort of people they are (kind, lazy, stupid, etc.).
7 What is the plot of 'The fire on the hill' (Module 4)? Make a list of the important things that happen.
8 Think about the plot for 'Saved!' Make a list of the things you want to happen in your story.

C Reading 2

Before reading: Share your ideas for your story, 'Saved!'

The process of writing a story

If you think of a good story, you will want other people to read it. Here is what you need to do to write a story that will be read by other people.

1 Decide what you want your story to be about. Who will the characters be? Where will it be set? What will happen? Share your ideas with a friend. Make notes about the ideas.
2 Complete a story plan. Use a plan like this:

Title:
Setting:
Characters:
Plot
Beginning:
Middle:
End:

3 Write your story. This is called 'the first draft'.
4 Read your story aloud to a friend or someone in your family. Talk about how you can make it better.
5 Make any changes you want to your story. You can take things out, write new parts or change the order of what you have written. This is the second draft.

6 Make sure there are no spelling or punctuation mistakes in your story.
- Check that you have spelt all the words correctly. Use a dictionary to help you.
- Put in all the full stops and capital letters.
- Put in all the other punctuation, like commas and question marks.

7 Hand your story in to your teacher for correction.

If you are pleased with your story, you can do a little more to make it even better

8 Read the corrections and advice your teacher has given you. Now write the story out again. Use your best handwriting, correct the mistakes and make any changes you want. This is the final version of your story.

9 Draw some pictures to illustrate your story.

10 Put the story on the classroom wall or submit it to the school magazine. This is called publishing the story. It means other people can read it.

D Comprehension 2

1 Put these stages in order, 1 to 10, according to the passage.
(a) Produce first draft
(b) Publish
(c) Teacher correction
(d) Produce second draft
(e) Illustrate
(f) Produce final version
(g) Think and make notes
(h) Read aloud and discuss
(i) Make a plan
(j) Check punctuation and spelling

2 Copy the story plan form and complete it for your story, 'Saved!'

3 Write the first draft of your story.

Word focus 🔍

Make sentences with these words:

experience   setting   character   plot   draft   version   illustrate   publish

E Grammar

1 Put in the correct preposition to complete the phrasal verbs.
(a) It's getting dark. Turn _____ the lights, please.
(b) We're all going out now. Please turn _____ the television.
(c) Our plane took _____ two hours late.
(d) I made _____ this story all by myself.
(e) The government has put _____ the price of petrol again.
(f) Do you think we'll get _____ the exams next term?
(g) We can pick you _____ on the way to school.
(h) Will you fill _____ this form, please?

2 Complete these sentences.
  (a) A cloud blocked out … (b) The thief broke in …
  (c) I had to put on … (d) The school had to turn away …
  (e) Lola went back … (f) He had to give up …
  (g) They went off … (h) My mother took my shoes back …

3 Make sentences using these phrasal verbs
  (a) call on (b) call for (c) leave for
  (d) depend on (e) look up to (f) look forward to

F Speech

1 Listen and say.
  (a) "Switch on the lights." "Switch them on."
  (b) "Look up the word in a dictionary." "Look it up."
  (c) "Fill in the form, please." "Fill it in."
  (d) "Please pick up Lola." "Pick her up."

2 Read the first draft of your story, 'Saved!' to other pupils. Listen to their stories. Give advice and suggestions to each other.

G Dictation

Look at the words below. They are all in the dictation you are going to do. Then listen to your teacher and write the paragraph.

draft   mistakes   spelling   punctuation   proof reading   dictionary

H Composition

1 Proof read Tunde's first draft of his story, 'Saved!' Correct the mistakes. He has made six spelling mistakes and he has missed out three full stops, one question mark and two capital letters.

We had been walkng for three days and were very tired Mercy had lost her shoes and her feet were cut. peter had falen and hurt his nee. I kept telling them to follow me because I was going to save them.

"Don't I always do what I say" I asked them

they were too tired to anser

Then, sudenly we pushed through some thick trees and saw a village in front of us. I new we were saved.

2 Complete your story, 'Saved!' Follow the procedure on pages 83 and 84.

19 Idioms and proverbs

A Reading

Before reading: Do you know what an idiom or proverb is? Do you know any examples?

This week our guide to the English language gives you a few tips on how to make your language a bit more colourful.

IDIOMS AND PROVERBS are part of the wealth of language. They give more colour and power to what you want to say.

You could say, "Don't judge a person by what he or she looks like." But how much better to say, "Don't judge a book by its cover"!

*'I was pulling your leg', means 'I was joking with you'. It is an **idiom**. The meaning of an idiom is different from the actual meaning of the words used.*

*'Children should be seen but never heard', is a **proverb**. Proverbs are old and popular sayings which contain some kind of traditional wisdom. Very often they give advice.*

Too many cooks spoil the broth.

Imagine that you are trying to do some work and lots of your friends are trying to help you. Instead of helping they are getting in the way and making a noise. Just say, "Too many cooks spoil the broth." They'll get the message! ('Broth' is an old word for soup.)

Many proverbs and idioms are very old, so we don't know who said them first and when. However, here are the origins of a few that you may know.

Saved by the bell

Schoolchildren often use this idiom when the bell for the end of the lesson is rung. It saves them from doing more work! But this is not the origin of the proverb. Nor is the bell at the end of a round in boxing, as many people think.

The first use was in England many years ago. The guard at one of the King's castles was arrested for sleeping when he was on duty. He was sentenced to have his head cut off. However, he said that he had been awake and at midnight he had heard the church bell ring thirteen times. The people in the village agreed that this had happened. So the guard was saved by the church bell.

It means to be saved from something unpleasant at the last moment.

An apple a day keeps the doctor away

This proverb is very old. The ancient Romans believed apples had magical powers to cure illness. In fact, apples do contain a lot of vitamins which are important for health.

Bury the hatchet

This idiom means to make up with a friend after a fight or argument. It comes from a tradition of native Americans (Indians). They used to bury their weapons – hatchets (which are like axes) – after fighting had finished.

The pen is mightier than the sword

In ancient England, people were not allowed to criticise the government. However, some people still did it. They wrote down their ideas and passed the papers around. The proverb is still true today; military power cannot stop people thinking and expressing their ideas in writing.

A close shave

This idiom comes from barbers who shaved men's beards as well as cut their hair. If they cut too close to the skin, they could cut the customer. Today it is used when someone just manages to avoid disaster.

Shed crocodile tears

When crocodiles open their mouths to eat, tears come out of their eyes. It looks as though they are crying! But, of course, they do not really feel sorry for the animal they are eating. So, when we say someone is 'shedding crocodile tears', it means that they are not truly sorry for what they have done.

B Comprehension

1 Where would you expect to read this text?
2 What is the purpose of the text?
3 Who is the usual audience for a text like this?
4 Why do we use idioms or proverbs when we speak and write?
5 What do proverbs usually do?
6 'Don't judge a book by its cover.' This means
   A Don't read books with bad covers,
   B Don't judge people by what they look like,
   C Don't judge people by the books they read.
7 'Too many cooks spoil the broth.' This means
   A Many hands make light work,
   B Too many people trying to help, don't help,
   C Many cooks don't know how to make good broth (soup).
8 Write example sentences to show the use of the *six* idioms and proverbs in the text.

Word focus

Make sentences with these words:

tip   wealth   origin   castle   ancient   criticise   military   shave   disaster

C Grammar

1 Look.

An **idiom** has a special meaning: it is made up of a number of words but its meaning is different from the ordinary meaning of the words. For example, 'to have cold feet' means to be afraid – it has nothing to do with cold feet.

2 Replace the underlined words with idioms from the box.

> getting on my nerves   hang on   pulling your leg   get a move on
> make it   what's the big deal

Busola: (a) <u>Hurry up,</u> we're going to be late.
Carama: Just (b) <u>wait a little</u>, I'll be there.
Busola: But if we don't go now, we won't (c) <u>arrive in time</u>.
Carama: So? (d) <u>Does it matter</u>? We can always go next week.
Busola: Now you're really (e) <u>making me angry</u>.
Carama: Don't worry, I'm only (f) <u>joking</u>. I'm ready, let's go.

3 Find the idioms in the following conversation. Explain what they mean.
   (a) *Shehu:* I don't think this is a good idea, I've got cold feet about it.
   (b) *Lekan:* Don't worry. I'll keep an eye on you when you go in.
   (c) *Shehu:* I'm not sure. We need to look at this from both sides.
   (d) *Lekan:* Well you really must make up your mind, I need to know.
   (e) *Shehu:* I'm sorry but I've had a change of heart. I'm not going to do it.
   (f) *Lekan:* If that's the case, then I wash my hands of you. Bye.
   (g) *Shehu:* That's fine. We have nothing in common anyway.

4 Match the idioms with their meanings. Write sentences using each idiom.
   (a) bury the hatchet   (i)   say something that is difficult to believe
   (b) down in the dumps   (ii) have hopes and dreams that will not come true
   (c) tell a tall story   (iii) be sad and depressed
   (d) make small talk   (iv) make polite conversation
   (e) have a heart of stone   (v)   settle an argument or fight
   (f) build castles in the air (vi) have no feeling or pity

D Speech

Say these tongue twisters. Start slowly and then say them faster and faster.

Say this sharply, say this sweetly,
Say this shortly, say this softly.
Say this sixteen times in succession.

While we were walking,
we were watching window washers
wash Washington's windows
with warm washing water.

Betty Botter bought some butter,
But, she said, the butter's bitter;
If I put it in my batter
It will make my batter bitter,
But a bit of better butter,
That would make my batter better.
So she bought a bit of butter
Better than her bitter butter,
And she put it in her batter
And the batter was not bitter.
So t'was better Betty Botter
Bought a bit of better butter.

bitter – tasting bad, not sweet
batter – a mixture of flour, milk and eggs for cooking
'twas – short form of 'it was'

E Dictation

Listen to your teacher and see if you can write this tongue twister. Then try saying it fast.

F Composition

1 Write a tongue twister. Choose one or two letters that can be difficult to say, such as p and b. Then think of words using the sounds, for example polar bear. Your tongue twister does not have to make good sense.

2 Write your diary for one day last week. Choose a day when something interesting happened.

When you write a diary, you make a record of what happened which was important to you.

• You don't write down everything that happened; only the interesting things.
• You can write down your thoughts and feelings.
• You can also write about interesting things you have learnt to help you remember. For example, you might want to record some of the idioms you have learnt this week.

A Reading

Fire *by* Shirley Hughes

Fire is a dragon
(Better beware),
Dangerous and beautiful
(Better take care).
Puffing out smoke
As soon as it's lit,
Licking up leaves,
Crackle and spit!
Sending up sparks
Into the sky
That hover a moment
And suddenly die.
Fire is a dragon,
Alive in the night;
Fiery dragon,
Glittering bright.

B Comprehension

1 'Fire is a dragon.' Is this
  A a simile,   B a metaphor,   C an idiom,   D a proverb,   E a synonym

2 Find words in the poem which mean
  (a) be careful,
  (b) blowing out small amounts (of air or smoke),
  (c) to make a sharp, low cracking sound,
  (d) tiny pieces of something burning,
  (e) to stay in the air without moving,
  (f) like a fire,
  (g) shining, sparkling.

3 The words 'beware' and 'care' rhyme. Which other pairs of words in the poem rhyme?

4 Recite the poem.

C Reading quiz

1 Find the answers in the Reading texts in Modules 11 to 19.

   (a) In 'The quarrel' (Module 11), why did the number of insects increase?

   (b) What symbol is used for the sound of the letters 'sh'?

   (c) What is this word /faɪə/?

   (d) What is the name of the process for taking salt out of sea water?

   (e) What does a marine biologist do?

   (f) What is the smallest fish?

   (g) What does the heart do?

   (h) What does HIV change to?

   (i) What is the **plot** of a story?

   (j) Complete this proverb, 'An apple a day ...'.

2 Write *ten* questions of your own about Reading texts 11 to 19.

3 Ask your questions.

Word focus

Make sentences with these words:

decrease   damage   extinct   observe   surface   organ   cure
protect   amazement   publish

D Grammar

Choose the answer that is closest in meaning.

1 'Sleep is like a blanket spread at night.' This is

   A an antonym,   B an idiom,   C a proverb,

   D a simile,   E a metaphor.

2 'I had to take back my new television.' This means

   A I returned the TV to the shop,

   B I bought a new TV,   C I broke my TV,

   D I left the TV at the shop,   E I took the TV from the shop.

3 'I'm looking forward to meeting her.' This means

   A I'm afraid of her,   B I know I'll like her,

   C I want to meet her,   D I know where to find her,

   E I'm looking for her.

4 'Lamide is down in the dumps.' This means

   A Lamide is ill,   B Lamide is sad,   C Lamide is angry,

   D Lamide is lost,   E Lamide is happy.

Complete the sentences. Choose the word or group of words that best fills the gap.

5 I don't like _____ medicines. They all taste terrible.
   A some   B something   C any
   D no   E none

6 I am thirsty but there's _____ to drink here.
   A nothing   B something   C anything
   D nobody   E none

7 If I were older, I _____ go to bed later.
   A will   B were   C would
   D want   E had

8 I hope you get _____ your exam next week.
   A on   B to   C in
   D up   E through

9 She writes stories and illustrates them herself. She is very _____.
   A create   B creature   C creation
   D creative   E recreate

Which word or phrase (A to E) is the most nearly opposite in meaning to the underlined word?

10 Dropping a radio can damage it.
    A break   B cure   C repair   D hurt   E manage

11 I'm going to spend all my money to buy Mum a present.
    A cost   B use   C buy   D sell   E save

12 The thief was found guilty and sent to prison.
    A judge   B innocent   C bad   D good   E sentenced

Which word or phrase (A to E) is the nearest in meaning to the underlined word?

13 Marine biologists like to explore under the sea.
    A search   B find   C swim   D go   E disappear

14 You must make the style of a letter appropriate to its audience.
    A content   B nice   C friendly   D formal   E suitable

15 You must protect small children.
    A feed   B play with   C watch   D listen to E take care of

Fun box

Did you know ...

... ants do not sleep and giraffes only sleep for five minutes a day?

... cats sleep 16 to 18 hours a day and a snail can sleep for three years?

... the bird of paradise can sleep upside down?

... dolphins sleep with one eye open?

E Speech

Look at the pictures. Tell the story.

F Dictation

Look at these words. Then listen to your teacher and write the paragraph.

mankind	earliest	achievement	discover	enable	danger	destroy
violent						

G Composition

1 Write the story of 'The stonecutter' you told in Speech above.

2 Imagine there was a fire near your home last week.

  (a) Write a report for the police. Record what happened.

  (b) Write your diary for the day of the fire. Describe what happened and what you thought.

93

21 The birthday party

A Reading 1

Before reading: What do you like to do at a birthday party?

Ugo's mum wanted to organise a surprise birthday party for Ugo at school, so she asked Ugo's friends to help.

On Monday morning, Zarat, Ugo's best friend, stood up in front of the class and asked, "Does anyone want to help organise Ugo's birthday party?"

"I do! Can I take care of the music?" asked Tunde.

"Me. I'll do the drinks,' shouted Sakiru.

"I'll be in charge of decorating the party room," said Omotola.

The children volunteered one by one.

"OK, thanks everyone. We'll all have to get together and plan, otherwise some things are going to be left undone," said Zarat.

"Why don't we do it now?" suggested Sakiru.

"All right, I've got some paper and a pen. Come round the table and let's make a plan," said Zarat.

The children gathered round the table. Zarat counted and was surprised that ten of her classmates had offered to help.

"Let me start by writing down the list of things to do, and then we'll appoint people to do the things. What do you think?" asked Zarat.

"OK," nodded all the children.

Zarat wrote down a long list of the things to do and then put the names of the people who offered to be in charge of them next to the items.

"Now that we have this organised, I think we should plan another meeting before the party," said Zarat.

"Why?" asked Tunde.

"To talk about how the plan is going. If we have any problems, we can sort them out before the day. What do you think?" asked Zarat.

"That's a good idea," they agreed.

"Let's make sure that we all do our bit so that the birthday goes smoothly on the day," said Sakiru.

"We shouldn't have any problems. Ugo's mum is there to support all of us," said Zarat.

"Zarat, can you invite Ugo's mum to our next meeting?" asked Bintu.

"That's a good idea! I'll invite her," agreed Zarat.

94

B Comprehension 1

1 Who is Ugo's best friend?
2 Why did the children need to make a plan?
3 How many children volunteered to help?
4 What did Zarat write on the plan?
5 Why did the children organise a second meeting?
6 Who did the children want at the second meeting?

C Reading 2

Before reading: What do you think the children will have organised?

At their next meeting, all the children reported what they had done. Tunde had asked his uncle to do the music for the party because he had lots of disco lights and many cds. Zarat had planned musical chairs, pass the parcel and musical statues.

For the party food, Ugo's mum had decided to prepare jollof rice, fried plantain and chicken. She had also bought six crates of soft drinks. Bintu said she and Ugo's mum were going to collect the cake a day before the party. Titi showed them the paper cups, plates and the plastic cutlery Ugo's mum had already bought.

Sakiru reported that the head teacher had agreed that they could use the chairs and tables in the hall. Omotola and her friends had started preparing posters to decorate the hall. Abdul said that he was helping Ugo's mum to do the party bags.

Emeka brought in a camera that he was going to use on the day and told everyone that Ugo's mum had also invited a photographer.

"Thank you for organising this. I'm very proud of you all," said Ugo's mother to the children. They were happy and looking forward to the party.

D Comprehension 2

Complete the record of what has been planned.

Ugo's party	What has been planned?
Drink	
Food	
Birthday cake	
Games	
Music	
Party bags	
Decorating	
Tables, chairs	
Plates, cups, etc.	
Photographs	

E Grammar

1 Look.

> The **-ing** form of the verb (the **gerund**) can be used as the subject of a sentence:
> **Decorating** the party room is fun.
> We can also use **to + infinitive**. This is more formal.
> **To make** mistakes is human.

2 Complete the sentences. Use the **gerund** or **to + infinitive** with the verbs in brackets.

<u>Watching</u> football is very exciting. (watch)

(a) _____ birthday parties is fun. (plan)

(b) _____ how to make birthday cakes is very useful. (know)

(c) _____ by plane is very fast. (travel)

(d) _____ presents is very good. (give)

(e) _____ your mistakes is important. (correct)

(f) _____ in big shops is very tiring. (shop)

(g) _____ TV is entertaining. (watch)

3 Complete the sentences in your own words.

(a) Writing …   (b) Sleeping …   (c) Listening …

(d) To teach …   (e) To travel …

4 Complete the sentences. Use the **-ing** form of the verb in the box.

> The **gerund** can be used as a subject, object or complement of a sentence.
> **Swimming** is tiring.   I love **swimming**.
> My favourite sport is **swimming**.

(a) _____ is bad for you.

(b) I go _____ on my bike every day.

(c) I love _____ birthday cake.

(d) My favourite sport is _____ .

(e) I like _____ by train.

(f) I hate _____ my clothes.

wash	travel	run
eat	smoke	cycle

F Speech

1 Imagine you and some friends want to organise a birthday party for a friend. Plan the party in a group. Make notes on who is in charge of each item and what they are going to do.

_____'s party		
Place:	Date:	Time:
	Who	What
Drink		
Food		
Birthday cake		
Games		
Music		
Party bags		
Decorating		
Tables, chairs		
Plates, cups, etc.		
Anything else		

2 Tell the class your group's plans for the party.

G Dictation

Look at the words below. They are all in the dictation you are going to do. Then listen to your teacher and write the paragraph.

celebrate	event	festival	annually	occasion	tradition	custom

H Composition

1 Write a report on your plans for the birthday party. Use the notes you made in Speech. Start:

_____'s party is going to be on _____ at _____.
_____ is going to organise the drink. She/He's going to

2 Write a letter to invite a friend to the party. Give the date, time, place and some details of what you are organising.

Fun box

Did you know ... the longest word in the English language is **pneumonoultramicroscopicsilicovolcanoconiosis**? It is an illness caused by dust from a volcano.

22 The prize-giving ceremony

A Reading 1

Before reading: What happens at your school's prize-giving ceremony?

The prize-giving ceremony of St Louis Primary School took place on Friday, 19 March, 20__, at 3pm in the school hall.

After the opening prayer, national anthem and school pledge, the Master of Ceremonies (MC) welcomed the parents and guests. He also introduced the chairman, Mr Femi Oguntolu, the proprietor of the school. The MC then called on the head teacher, Mrs Omali, to give her report to the school.

After her speech, the headmistress used a slide projector to show the audience some pictures of the daily routine of the school. The children enjoyed this very much.

Following this, the school dramatic society performed two short plays and the music society sang various songs.

Then, the chairman presented gifts to some of the staff. Mallam Kolo and Mrs Ume were given special presents for their 15 and 20 years of service to the school. Mrs Bashir was given a farewell gift as she will be leaving the school at the end of the term to take up another post in Abuja.

Mr Oguntolu and the headmistress presented the prizes to the students. They gave prizes to pupils for academic, sports and extracurricular activities. Halema Garba received the Michael Olusola Aregbesola Award for the student showing the most interest in the search for knowledge and information. Ugo Ukpai received the Peter Bala Memorial Prize for the Best All Round Sports Student and Zarat Abubakar won the Ajakaye Drawing Prize for Art. Toni Chukwu received the Rosemary Adaramola prize for the most well-behaved student.

The head boy then gave a short speech about the activities in the school year.

Finally, the head girl moved a vote of thanks to the chairman, the headmistress and staff of the school. The Chief Imam led the closing prayers.

The evening was a great success.

B Comprehension 1

1 What type of ceremony is this report about?
2 Who was the chairman of the ceremony?
3 Who introduced him?
4 What did the MC do next?
5 Why did Mrs Bashir receive a gift?
6 Who received a prize for being the best sports student?
7 What happened after the prize-giving?
8 Who moved the vote of thanks?

C Reading 2

Before reading: What do you think the headmistress said in her speech?

This was the headmistress's speech to the school.

"In my ten years in this school, I have seen new buildings, a new library and many new teachers. All these changes are part of a plan to give pupils the best chance for a good start in life. I am happy to be part of this wonderful school.

I always encourage my pupils to believe in themselves. In addition, I tell them that our great school gives them the same opportunities as children in other parts of the world.

The most important purpose of any primary school is to give its pupils a good education. This means they can get into good secondary schools and then, later, into a fine university. This will help them to have happy lives and earn good money in years to come. Last year, most of my pupils gained admission to the best secondary schools in the state.

I thank all of you, each in your own way, for the input you make to the success of the school. We have a hardworking staff, the pupils are well-behaved and the parents are reliable.

I thank this year's final grade pupils and their parents for their kind gift of a statue, to be erected in front of the school. I also thank the Parents Association for giving the school 100,000 naira, which we plan to use for a bigger computer room."

D Comprehension 2

1 How long has Mrs Omali been headmistress of the school?
2 What changes have happened in that time?
3 What does Mrs Omali say is the main purpose of a primary school?
4 Why does she think this?

5 '... the input you make to the success of the school.' This means
   A what you do to make the school successful,
   B what you pay to make the school successful,
   C what you make for the school is successful.

6 '...a statue, to be erected ...' This means the statue
   A has been put up,   B will be put up,   C is being put up now.

7 What have the Parents Association given to the school?

8 What is the gift going to be used for?

Word focus 🔍

Make sentences with these words:

proprietor   service   academic   extracurricular   reliable   statue   erect

E Grammar

1 Look.

> Use **too** + adjective/adverb or **not** + adjective/adverb + **enough** to describe
> something which is not right.
>
>   *This traffic moves **too** slowly.*   *This pencil is **not** sharp **enough**.*

2 Complete the sentences. Use **too** or **not ... enough** and the adjective or adverb.
   (a) I'm not going to the prize-giving ceremony. I'm _____. (ill)
   (b) You have to rewrite your homework. It's _____. (good)
   (c) We can't do our homework. It's _____. (difficult)
   (d) I can't understand Mr Aderigbe very well. He talks _____. (quickly)
   (e) My shoes hurt. They're _____. (big)
   (f) I don't think he'll pass his exam, he does _____ work _____. (hard)

3 Look.

> Use **very** + adjective/adverb to make it stronger.
>   *It's **very** hot.*   *She runs **very** slowly.*
> Use **too** + adjective/adverb to say something is not right.
>   *It's **too** hot. (I am uncomfortable.)*
>   *She runs **too** slowly. (She won't win the race.)*

4 Write a sentence about each picture on page 101. Use the words in the box.

> very salty   too salty   very hot   too hot
> very expensive   too expensive

100

5 Look.

stronger ——————————————————————————————————————→

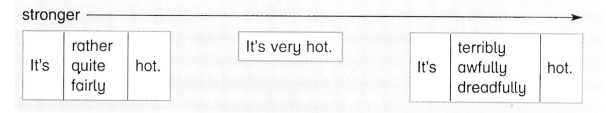

| It's | rather quite fairly | hot. |

It's very hot.

| It's | terribly awfully dreadfully | hot. |

6 Make sentences using the following.

(a) rather cold
(b) awfully worried
(c) very tired
(d) quite exhausted
(e) terribly angry
(f) fairly late

F Speech

1 Read aloud the headmistress's speech on page 99.

2 Imagine that you are the head girl or head boy of the St Louis Primary School. Give a short speech at the prize-giving.

- Talk about the activities in the school (trips, competitions, etc.).
- Thank the teachers and staff for their help.

G Dictation

Look at the words below. They are all in the dictation you are going to do. Then listen to your teacher and write the paragraph.

| chairman | proprietor | pleased | ceremony | introduce | occasion |

H Composition

1 Imagine you are at the school-leaving party. All your school friends are there. Write a speech to give at the end of the party.

- You are talking to friends so the speech does not need to be as formal as the headmistress's speech you read in Speech.
- Write about your memories of the school and your friends.
- Write a little about the future.

Read your speech aloud.

2 Write a short report on the school-leaving party.

23 The twins

A Reading 1

Before reading: What are twins? Do you know any twins? Do you know any stories about twins?

"What?" said the chief angrily. "You do not want to kill them? Go away from the village and never come back, or I shall kill you together with your children."

These were the last words that the couple had heard spoken in their village. They left the village the same day and never returned, just as their chief had ordered. Now the boys wanted to go to the village. Sadly, the parents had to explain to their sons the old custom that had driven them away from their home.

The couple had lived happily in the village of Serki all their lives. They were born there, had got married there and had hoped to die there. But then the woman became pregnant. What started as a cause for joy turned to sorrow when she gave birth. She produced twins, both boys. They were beautiful babies and were identical.

Their parents were very happy and very sad at the same time. You will ask, "Why?" Because there was a custom in Serki: to kill twins. They were thought to bring misfortune to the village and its people. The chief of Serki said, "Those baby twins must die!" But their father and mother did not want to kill their sons. So the family went into exile.

For many years, the family lived in the forest. Life was not easy there. The couple had to work hard to make a living and it was a lonely life away from the company of other villagers. However, the twins grew up strong and, as soon as they were old enough, they helped their father and mother with their work. In time, they became good and handsome young men.

B Comprehension 1

1 What was the custom in Serki?
2 What was the reason for this custom?
3 Why was the chief angry with the couple?
4 Why did the couple have to leave the village?
5 What happened to them after they left the village?

6 'What started as a cause for joy turned to sorrow...' This means

   A they were sad but became happy,

   B they were happy but became sad,

   C they were happy and sad at the same time.

7 The babies were identical. This means the babies

   A looked the same,   B were joined together,   C were unhappy.

8 '... the family went into exile.' This means

   A they went to another country,

   B they all died,

   C they went away from their homes to another place.

C Reading 2

Before reading: Look at the pictures. What do you think will happen?

   Then one day the twins found a man in the forest. He was dying. They tried to help him but he said, "Don't help me. If you want to help, go and fight for my people. I come from Serki. There's a war on there now. We fought bravely, but the enemy is stronger than we are." With these words he died.

   The twins wanted to go to Serki and help to fight but their father and mother were against it. They told the boys, "The chief doesn't want you there. He wanted to kill you when you were small children."

   However, the twins still wanted to go and help. They said, "Serki is our traditional home. We must help our people."

   So the boys went to Serki and helped to fight against the enemy. They fought bravely and helped the people to win the war.

   The chief called for a big feast to celebrate the victory. The twins were there and were praised for their help. One man stood up and said, "There are two young men here, two brothers. They are very brave soldiers but we don't know who they are."

The twins' uncle was at the feast, too. He recognised his nephews. He said to the chief, "Remember the baby twins born in the village eighteen years ago. You ordered their parents to kill them. They chose instead to go into exile. These are the same twins come back to help us."

The chief called the boys to him and asked them to forgive him. Then he sent the twins back to their parents with many presents and a letter in which he asked them to come back and live in the village.

From that day on, the tradition of killing twins in Serki was abandoned.

D Comprehension 2

The story below is not told in the order in which it happened. Put the sentences in order to make a summary of the events in the order in which they happened.

(a) The chief ordered the twins to be killed, to follow the tradition of Serki.

(b) When they were young men, the twins found a dying warrior who told them to go and help the people of Serki who were at war.

(c) Twin boys were born.

(d) The couple refused to kill their children and left the village.

(e) The boys did return and helped Serki win the war.

(f) The wife became pregnant.

(g) The chief learnt who the two warriors were. He apologised to them and the tradition of killing twins was stopped.

(h) The old couple told the twins what had happened and asked them not to return to Serki.

(i) A couple got married and lived happily in Serki.

(j) The twins grew up with their parents in the forest.

Word focus 🔍

Make sentences with these words:

drive away   identical   misfortune   exile   company   enemy
recognise   forgive   abandon

E Grammar

1 Find *five* adverbs and *ten* adjectives in the story of 'The twins'.

Adjectives describe a noun (a person or a thing).
Adverbs describe a verb.

2 Look.

We make comparisons with adverbs in a similar way to how we make comparisons with adjectives.

Some short adverbs (**early**, **late**, **fast**, **hard**, **near**, **soon**) use suffixes **-er** and **-est**.

*I get up **earlier** than my brother.*   *Lola lives the **nearest** to school.*

Other adverbs use **more** and **the most**.

*The chief spoke **more angrily** with every minute that passed.*
*The twins fought **the most bravely** of all the warriors.*

There are some irregular comparative adverbs.

well/better/the best   *badly/worse/the worst*

3 Ask and answer. Find someone who

   (a) gets up earlier than you,   (b) goes to bed later than you,

   (c) writes more neatly than you,   (d) sings better than you.

4 Complete the sentences about the pictures. Use comparative adverbs.

(a) He should drive _____.   (b) He needs to run _____.

(c) She wants to live _____ to the sea.   (d) They should play _____.

5 Write sentences. Use the words and **than**.

    My father drives/fast/my mother

    My father drives faster than my mother.

(a) I work/hard/my brother.

(b) Joke writes/neatly/Funmi.

(c) Our class behaves/well/class 5C.

(d) Uthman talks/loudly/Ibrahim.

(e) Udoma speaks English/badly/Johnson.

(f) I talk to people/politely/my little sister.

F Speech

1 Hold a class debate on the motion:

'We should respect our traditions and customs.'

(a) Work in groups. Prepare all your ideas for the topic.

(b) Listen as your teacher explains how to organise the debate.

- *Proposers:* prepare a speech to propose the motion. Think of all the ideas you can to support it.
- *Opposers:* prepare a speech to oppose the motion. Think of all the ideas you can against it.
- *Rest of class:* think of questions to ask the speakers.

2 Act out an interview. Work in pairs.

- One of you is a character from the story, 'The twins'. It is ten years after the twins returned to the village.
- One of you is a reporter for a magazine. You want to write an article about traditions and how they change. You want to know what happened and why twins are no longer killed in the village.

G Dictation

Look at the words below. They are all in the dictation you are going to do.
Then listen to your teacher and write the paragraph.

traditionally	population	nations	developed	factories	residents
ancestors					

H Composition

1 Write a composition giving your view on traditions and customs. You can use some of the ideas discussed in the debate.

You can use some of the following phrases:

In my opinion ...   *I believe ...*   *Another point ...*
Furthermore ...   *Finally ...*   *To conclude ...*

2 Write the interview you acted out in Speech.

Reporter: May I ask a few questions about customs in your village?
Villager:

Fun box

Did you know ...

... for every 100 girls born in the world, 106 boys are born?

24 Famous Nigerians

A Reading 1

Before reading: What do you know about Dr Nnamdi Azikiwe?

Nnamdi Azikiwe was born in Zungeru in Niger State on 16 November, 1904. He attended schools in Onitsha, Calabar and Lagos. After he graduated from the Wesleyan Boys' High School at the top of his class in 1925, he went to study in the USA. He became the first Nigerian to study in an American University.

In 1934, Azikiwe, popularly known as 'Zik', became the editor of the *African Morning Post* in Ghana. He married Flora Ogoegbunam in 1936 and had three sons and one daughter. In 1937, he founded the *West African Pilot* newspaper in Nigeria.

He worked for many years, both as a journalist and as a politician, to end British control of Nigeria. When Nigeria gained independence in 1960, he became the Governor-General of the country. Three years later, Nnamdi Azikiwe became the first President of Nigeria.

He was a national hero who could influence large crowds with his powerful speeches. He travelled frequently to other countries to represent Nigeria. He held the traditional title of 'Owelle of Onitsha'. He also wrote over a dozen books on African independence and other topics. He died in 1996, at the age of 91, after a long illness.

B Comprehension 1

1　How old was Azikiwe when he went to the USA?
2　What was surprising about these studies?
3　What did people usually call him?
4　How old was he when he got married?
5　'… he founded the West African Pilot newspaper …'. This means
　　A he edited the newspaper,　　B he bought the newspaper,
　　C he started the newspaper.
6　What was his main aim as a politician before 1960?
7　In which year did he become President?
8　'He … could influence large crowds …'. This means
　　A he could make people change their minds,
　　B he could call together many people,
　　C he could talk to many people at the same time.

C Reading 2

Before reading: What do you know about Alhaji Tafawa Balewa?

Alhaji Sir Abubakar Tafawa Balewa was the first Prime Minister of Nigeria in 1960. He was a great leader who wanted to unite all the people of the country to make Nigeria strong and successful.

He was born in 1912 in a northern village. His family was not rich but he was a clever student. He studied to be a teacher at Katsina College. He taught for three years and then went to study at the University of London.

On his return to Nigeria, he became a politician. He spoke well and was a popular leader. He became a member of the Northern Region House of Assembly in 1947 and then, in 1951, he was elected to the House of Representatives.

He had many important government jobs and in 1957 he was made Prime Minister of the Nigerian Federation. When Nigeria became independent in 1960, he continued to be Prime Minister. At that time, the Queen of England made him a knight, with the title, 'Sir' to thank him for his good service to his country. He was killed in 1966 in a military coup.

Not only was he a great leader, politician and teacher, but he was also a writer. His story, *Shaihu Umar*, is about a boy captured by slave traders.

D Comprehension 2

1 Where in Nigeria did Balewa study to be a teacher?
2 Where else did he study?
3 When did he become a politician?
4 What happened in 1951?
5 What job did he do from 1957?
6 What job did he have after Independence?
7 When did he die?
8 He is famous as a great political leader. What else did he do?

Word focus 🔍 Make sentences with these words:
found   politician   influence   frequently   represent   leader   unite   elect

E Grammar

1 Look.

To talk about something which is possible, or likely to happen, use
> **If + present simple tense, will + infinitive**
> *If you read 'Shaihu Umar', you will enjoy it.*

To talk about something which is unlikely to happen, use
> **If + past simple tense, would + infinitive**
> *If I became President of Nigeria, I would make school holidays longer.*

To talk about something that is impossible, which cannot happen, use
> **If + past perfect tense, would have + past participle**
> *If I had worked harder last year, I would have passed my exam.*

2 Match the two parts to make sentences.

(a) If you work hard,
(b) If we waste water,
(c) If I spoke French,
(d) If I were a writer,
(e) If we had known it was your birthday,
(f) If I had met Alhaji Tafawa Balewa,

(i) I would go to Togo.
(ii) I would have been very happy.
(iii) I will buy you a present.
(iv) there won't be enough for everyone.
(v) I would want to write like Chinua Achebe.
(vi) we would have organised a birthday party.

3 Complete the sentences.

(a) If I live to be sixty, …
(b) If I lived to be a hundred, …
(c) If I had lived one hundred years ago, …
(d) If it rains tomorrow, …
(e) If it snowed tomorrow, …
(f) If it had snowed yesterday, …

F Speech

1 Talk for one minute on 'My hero'.

- Choose someone who you admire. This can be a leader, a sportsman or woman, a singer, musician, actor, etc.
- Give as many facts about your hero as you can.
- Say why you like the person.

2 Read and recite this poem.

Penfriend *by* Pauline Stewart

I'm writing my friend a letter.
She lives across the sea
I hope she'll come over
and visit my family.
I wonder what sights she sees
I wonder what she does.
I suppose really
she's more or less like us.
All kinds of people
live in the world today,
I wonder if they wrote to me
exactly what they'd say?

G Dictation

Look at the words below. They are all in the dictation you are going to do.
Then listen to your teacher and write the paragraph.

library   biography   autobiography   famous   successful

H Composition

1 Write the biography of Chief Obafemi Awolowo. Use the notes below.
- Political leader and Yoruba chief, popularly called 'Awo'
- Born 6 March, 1909 in Ikenne, Ijebu Remo
- Educated at Baptist Boys' High School, Abeokuta, Ogun State and Wesley College, Ibadan
- Worked as a trader and journalist
- 1939: started part-time studies
- 1944: gained a university degree and went to study law in London
- Founded the Egbe Omo Oduduwa society
- 1947: qualified in law and returned to Nigeria
- Became Premier of Western Nigeria
- Died in 1987

2 Imagine you have a penfriend, just like the author of the poem above. Write a letter to tell him or her about you, your family and your life.

A Reading 1

Before reading: Look at the picture of the man. Who is it? What did he do?

Mvezo is a tiny village on the banks of the Mbashe River in the Transkei. It is surrounded by rolling hills and fertile valleys. A thousand rivers and streams keep the countryside green even in winter. ... It was here that I was born on 18 July 1918.

... My father, Gadla Henry Mphakanyiswa, was a chief and a member of the Thembu royal family. Although my father could not read or write, he was a wise man who knew much about the history of our people. He was a trusted adviser to the king.

When I was born my father gave me the name Rolihlahla, which means "pulling the branch of a tree". Put more simply, it means "trouble-maker".

He could not have known what lay ahead of me. But looking back at all the "trouble" I have caused, it was a good name.

My mother, Nosekeni Fanny, was the third of my father's four wives. Together they had four children, three daughters and myself.

Altogether, my father had 13 children, four boys and nine girls. I was the youngest of the boys.

When I was still a baby, my father suffered a great hardship which was to change our lives forever. He lost his chieftainship — all because of an ox.

One day, a man complained to the magistrate that one of my father's oxen had strayed on to his land. The magistrate ordered my father to appear before him. But my father, who was a proud man, refused to go to the magistrate. ...

My father paid a heavy price for not obeying the magistrate. He not only lost his chieftainship, but he lost his cattle and land as well. We had no choice but to leave our home.

The move away from Mvezo took me to a place where I was to spend some of the happiest years of my life.

B Comprehension 1

1 Where was Mandela born?
2 What were the names of his parents?
3 Was his father well educated?
4 Why does Mandela think Rolihlahla is a good name for him?
5 Why did the magistrate want to see Mandela's father?
6 Why didn't Mandela's father appear before the magistrate?
7 What happened as a result?
8 'My father paid a heavy price for not obeying the magistrate.' This means
   A he suffered a lot because he didn't do what he was told,
   B he paid a lot of money because he didn't do what he was told,
   C he paid a lot to buy the oxen from the magistrate.

C Reading 2

Before reading: This is part of the autobiography of Nelson Mandela. What do you know about him?

Both my parents were religious, but in different ways. My father believed in Qamata, the God of his fathers and the great spirit of the Xhosa people. My mother, on the other hand, became a Christian and baptised me into the Methodist Church.

My parents were friendly with two brothers in the village, George and Ben Mbekela. They too were Christians and had a strong belief in the importance of education. ...

I was just seven years old when George visited my mother and said, "Your son is a clever young fellow. He should go to school."

My mother kept quiet. No one in our family had ever gone to school before. But she told my father what George had said. My father decided to give to his son what he had never had himself — an education. ...

On my first day of school, my father took a pair of his trousers and cut them at the knee. He told me to put them on and tied a piece of string around the waist. This was the first pair of trousers I ever owned.

Up until then, I had only worn a blanket, like all the other boys in the village. I must have looked very funny in my father's trousers, but I could not have been more proud.

I not only got a new pair of trousers on my first day at school — I got a new name too. In those days, black children were given white names at school because it was more "civilised". My teacher called me Nelson.

D Comprehension 2

1 In what ways were Mandela's parents religious?
2 Why were George and Ben Mbekela important in Mandela's life?
3 Why did George want Mandela to go to school?
4 What did Mandela's mother say?
5 What did Mandela's father decide?
6 What did Mandela wear before he started school?
7 What did he wear to school on the first day?
8 What else did Mandela get when he started school?

Word focus 🔍 Make sentences with these words:

rolling   fertile   valley   troublemaker   hardship   stray   magistrate
obey   baptise   waist

E Grammar

1 Look.

In the first conditional, other modal verbs sometimes replace **will**.
*If you are good, I **might** buy you a new T-shirt.*
*I **can** go to the party tonight if I help Mother this afternoon.*
*If you are not better tomorrow, you **should** go to the hospital.*

2 Match the two parts to make sentences.

(a) If you don't drink for a long time,
(b) If it is very hot,
(c) We should leave for school now
(d) You could get ill
(e) If I get some money,
(f) My father says I can have a new bicycle,

(i)   if I help him during the holidays.
(ii) if you drink dirty water.
(iii) you might die.
(iv) I might buy a video.
(v)   we may go swimming.
(vi) if we don't want to arrive late.

3 Choose **If** or **When** to start the sentences. Then complete them in your own words.

> Use **when** instead of **if** when you are certain something will happen.
> *When I go home, I will do my homework.* (You know you will go home.)
> *When the sun sets, it gets dark.* (You know the sun will set.)

(a) _____ it gets dark, ... (b) _____ I become President, ...

(c) _____ I pass my exam, ... (c) _____ I wake up tomorrow, ...

(e) _____ I leave this school, ... (f) _____ you change your mind, ...

4 Rewrite these sentences. Use **unless**.

> Use **unless** to mean 'if not'.
> *I won't go to school tomorrow* **unless** *I feel better.* (= if I don't feel better)
> **Unless** *he wore trousers, Mandela couldn't go to school.* (= if he didn't wear trousers)

I won't help you if you don't help me.
I won't help you unless you help me.

(a) You can't watch this film if you are not old enough.

(b) I don't run to school if I'm not really late.

(c) If you don't have a ticket, you can't get on a plane.

(d) If I don't go to see my grandfather on Saturday, I'll be at home.

(e) I always watch TV at night if I don't have any homework to do.

F Speech

1 Give a short talk about 'Myself'.

- Give some facts about yourself – where you were born, when, etc.
- Give some interesting information – what you like doing, eating, etc.

2 Read and say.

(a) Choose these shoes, not those shoes

(b) five very fine vases

(c) a black bird at a dirty dish

(d) a baby baboon with pepper and pawpaw

(e) that thief there thinks Thursdays are for theft

(f) red lorry, yellow lorry, red lorry, yellow lorry

G Dictation

Look at the words below. They are all in the dictation you are going to do. It is another part of Mandela's autobiography, *A long walk to freedom*. Then listen to your teacher and write the paragraph.

millions
South Africans
polling station
cast
vote
democratic election
patiently
choice

H Composition

1 Write your autobiography.
   * Include some facts – where you were born, when, etc.
   * Include some description of where you were born or grew up. (Look again at Mandela's description of Mvezo.)
   * Include some interesting information. (Look again at Mandela's description of his first day at school.)
2 Write your diary for one day in the last week.

Fun box

Did you know ...

... Nelson Mandela spent 27 years in prison before he was elected President of South Africa? At his trial he said,

> I have cherished the ideal of a democratic and free society in which all persons live together in harmony and with equal opportunities. It is an ideal which I hope to live for and to achieve. But if needs be, it is an ideal for which I am prepared to die.

26 Life at secondary school

A Reading 1

Before reading: You will soon be going to secondary school. In what ways do you think it will be different from primary school?

Sanni was busy drawing small diagrams on a chart. Zarat couldn't keep quiet any longer.

"What are you doing?" she asked her brother.

"I'm making a weather chart," replied Sanni. "We measure the temperature and rainfall every day at school and then I record the information for homework."

"That's interesting! It must be cool to be at secondary school. I can't wait to start next year! Is it very different to primary school?" asked Zarat.

"Yes, some things are different," said Sanni.

"So, what's different?" Zarat asked.

"Well, there are different teachers for different subjects," said Sanni.

"How many teachers do you have, then?" she asked.

"Let me think." Sanni closed his eyes as he thought. "I have twelve teachers."

"Twelve! That's a lot," said Zarat.

"Yes, twelve teachers for twelve subjects," Sanni replied.

"What else is different?" demanded Zarat.

"You're treated more like an adult," said Sanni. "Teachers expect you to do your homework without being told every day, to arrive in lessons on time and to behave responsibly at all times."

"Is that hard?" asked Zarat.

"No," he said. "You just have to be sensible."

"So, do you enjoy it?" Zarat wanted to know.

"Yes," said Sanni enthusiastically. "You get to do work that is more fun – like science experiments! We are shown how to use chemicals, Bunsen burners and all kinds of different equipment! Then, in art, we use charcoal, paints, chalk, and we even have models to draw!"

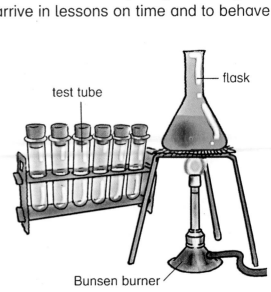

test tube

flask

Bunsen burner

"Models? We have to draw using our imaginations, which is a lot harder," said Zarat.

"No, it's not. It's much harder drawing something you can see and to make it look exactly the way it should," replied Sanni.

"So everything is more difficult! It's going to be too difficult for me!" said Zarat nervously.

B Comprehension 1

1 What was Sanni doing before Zarat started talking?
2 What was he recording?
3 Does Sanni think secondary school is very different to primary school?
4 Why does Sanni have twelve different teachers?
5 What do secondary school teachers expect their students to do?
6 What does Sanni like about secondary school?
7 How does Zarat feel about going to secondary school?
8 How do you feel about going to secondary school?

C Reading 2

Before reading: What do you think the best thing about going to a secondary school will be?

"No, don't worry! I'm sure that you'll be fine," Sanni told his sister. "You'll do very well and you'll make more friends and have a lot of fun. For example, you can go on school trips and spend a few days there!"

"What? Our trips last a day or less than a day …," said Zarat quietly.

"Don't worry," said Sanni. "That's because kids of ten or less can't take care of themselves that well. Just wait until you're at secondary school and you're as old as me."

"Sanni, you're only fifteen, you're not twenty," laughed Zarat.

"I'm older than you, and I know about secondary school," said Sanni.

"So, what else should I know?" asked Zarat.

Sanni thought for a moment. "The school is much bigger, you'll have more books, there are more school rules and the discipline is a lot stricter than at primary school."

"Science is my best subject. I hope I continue to enjoy it in secondary school," Zarat said.

"You'll do a lot more of it. In secondary school it'll be divided into three parts," said Sanni.

"What do you mean?" asked Zarat.

"It'll be divided into chemistry, biology and physics," Sanni explained.

117

"Are we expected to do them all?" Zarat asked.

"Yes, you do them all at first, then later you can choose which you want to do," said Sanni.

"What about sports?" asked Zarat. "I love sports."

"Yes, we do lots of different sports and we play against all the other secondary schools in the region. But now," said Sanni firmly, "I need to finish my homework."

"Can I help you?" asked Zarat. "I'm good at drawing diagrams."

D Comprehension 2

1 What does Sanni think Zarat will enjoy at secondary school?
2 What is different between school trips at primary and secondary school?
3 Why does Sanni think primary school trips are short?
4 What else does Sanni tell his sister about secondary school?
5 What is different about science at secondary school?
6 Do secondary school students study all three science subjects?

> **Word focus** Make sentences with these words:
> diagram   chart   responsibly   nervously   trip   discipline   strict   divide

E Grammar

1 Look.

Question-tags

*Secondary school is good, **isn't it**?   He can't swim, **can he**?*

• We use question tags when we think we know the answer to the question.
• We use them mostly in speaking, not usually in writing.
• We use the auxiliary verb from the main part of the sentence in the tag.
• If the main part of the sentence is positive, we use a negative tag. If the main part of the sentence is negative, we use a positive tag.

| + AUXILIARY , | – TAG | – AUXILIARY, | + TAG |

*We **will** see you again, **won't we**?   They **haven't** arrived yet, **have** they?*

2 Complete with the correct tag.
(a) You are going to school today, ...
(b) We can't stop, ...
(c) You aren't going to forget, ...
(d) We mustn't be late, ...
(e) I'm making too much noise, ...
(f) It will be ready soon, ...
(g) She hasn't got a brother, ...
(h) It won't be long now, ...

3 Look.

When there is no auxiliary in the main part of the sentence, we make the tag with the verb **do**.

> They go to secondary school, **don't they**?
> She likes science, **doesn't she**?

If the main verb is in the past tense, we make the tag with the past tense of **do**.

> He started secondary school last year, **didn't he**?

4 Complete the sentences. Use a tag from the box.

do we?	didn't she?	didn't you?	don't we?	did they?	do I?
don't you?	did you?	doesn't he?	did it?		

Questions to which you think the answer is **yes**.

(a) You like school, ...
(b) He enjoys science, ...
(c) You saw them, ...
(d) We often read together, ...
(e) Tunde asked a lot of questions, ...

Questions to which you think the answer is **no**.

(f) You didn't like me, ...
(g) They didn't do their exercise, ...
(h) The dog didn't bark, ...
(i) We don't need to help, ...
(j) I don't eat enough vegetables, ...

5 Complete with the correct tag.

(a) We can't hear from here ...
(b) Ugo doesn't like singing, ...
(c) He speaks too quietly, ...
(d) You are never happy, ...
(e) They love juju music, ...
(f) We didn't use to live here, ...
(g) You saw them, ...
(h) It was easy, ...
(i) Tunde found the answer, ...
(j) It wasn't difficult, ...

F Speech

1 Look.

We usually use a question-tag question when we know the answer. They are not real questions. We expect the listener to agree with us. We say them with falling intonation:

> Science is your best subject, isn't it?

Sometimes we use question-tag questions as real questions. We say them with rising intonation:

> Science is your best subject, isn't it?

2 Listen to your teacher say these. Write them and mark the falling or rising intonation.

   (a) Secondary schools are very big, aren't they?
   (b) Zarat's nervous, isn't she?
   (c) Sanni's a secondary school pupil, isn't he?
   (d) The secondary school isn't far from here, is it?
   (e) They work hard at secondary school, don't they?
   (f) Zarat can draw good diagrams, can't she?

3 Say the questions above with falling or rising intonation.

4 You are going to interview each other. Work in groups of four.

   (a) Imagine you are teachers at a secondary school. You are going to ask primary school pupils who want to study at your school some questions. Write *six* questions to ask. For example:

   What is your favourite subject?   Are you good at sports?

   (b) Take it in turns to be interviewed. Three of you ask the questions. The pupil being interviewed must answer all the questions clearly.

G Dictation

Look at the words below. They are all in the dictation you are going to do. Then listen to your teacher and write the paragraph.

| scientists | biology | chemistry | chemicals | physics | occur naturally |

H Composition

1 Write a record of the interview you did in Speech. Write the *six* questions you were asked and your answers.

   Interviewer: What is your favourite subject?
   Me: English is my favourite subject but I also like maths and science.

2 Imagine you have started at a new secondary school. Write a letter to tell a friend about it.

Fun box

Did you know ...

... if monkeys eat too many green bananas, their tongues and eyes will turn green?

120

27 Computers

A Reading 1

Before reading: Have you ever used a computer? What did you do on it?

Computers are everywhere. When people talk about computers it can sound very complicated, but it doesn't have to be.

What does a computer look like?

Most computers you will see are personal computers (PC). They fit onto a desk and one person can use them.

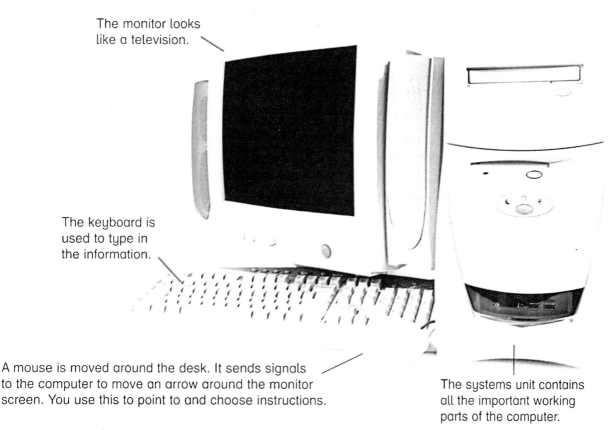

The monitor looks like a television.

The keyboard is used to type in the information.

A mouse is moved around the desk. It sends signals to the computer to move an arrow around the monitor screen. You use this to point to and choose instructions.

The systems unit contains all the important working parts of the computer.

What is a computer?

A computer is a machine which works with information (called data). Information is put into the computer with a set of instructions (a program). The program tells the computer what to do with the data. It then gives the results.

Computers work very fast. An English teacher called William Shanks once did a very difficult mathematical calculation. It took him 28 years! A modern computer can do it in a few seconds. It will also show that he made a mistake in his calculation!

However, a computer cannot think for itself. If there is any mistake with the data or program, then the results will be nonsense.

121

B Comprehension 1

1 What does PC mean?
2 How big is a personal computer?
3 What do you use to type in the information?
4 What do you look at to see the information?
5 Which part does all the work?
6 What do you use to point an arrow on the monitor?
7 What is a computer program?
8 What will happen if a computer is given data which contains a mistake?

C Reading 2

Before reading: What do people use computers for?

What are computers used for?

They are used for thousands of things:

- They are used in offices, banks, shops and science laboratories to do mathematical calculations.
- They are very useful for writing. If you make a mistake while you are writing, it is very easy to correct it. The computer can even check your spelling and grammar. This book was written using one.
- A computer can be attached to a telephone line. This allows you to send what you write to another computer, maybe thousands of kilometres away – this is called e-mail.
- Many thousands of computers can be joined together. This is called the Internet, or World Wide Web (www). You can use this to get the information on other computers onto your computer. Many schools, colleges and universities now have computers, and students use them to do their homework.

What is the future of computers?

Computers will continue to get smaller and to work faster. There are already computers you can hold in your hand. Mobile phones have computers and you can send e-mail and use the Internet from them.

Keyboards may disappear from computers. In the future, you will be able to talk to a computer. You will tell it the information and what you want it to do. It will understand your voice and do what it is told.

Computers will also continue to get cheaper and have more uses. One day they will become common even in poor rural areas.

More and more jobs will require the ability to use a computer. It is therefore useful to learn how to use them at school.

D Comprehension 2

1 Match the words from the text with their meanings.

(a) computer
(b) data
(c) computer program
(d) calculation
(e) e-mail
(f) internet

(i) something that you work out by using numbers
(ii) a set of instructions for a computer
(iii) a link between thousands of computers to exchange information
(iv) information
(v) a machine that does things with information
(vi) electronic mail – a way of sending messages from computer to computer

2 Computers will become
A smaller, faster and more expensive,
B smaller, slower and cheaper,
C smaller, faster and cheaper.

3 In the future, how will people be able to give information to a computer if there is no keyboard?

4 Why is it useful to learn how to use computers at school?

Word focus 🔍

Make sentences with these words:
complicated   modern   nonsense   attach   disappear   require

E Grammar

1 Look.

Compare the active and passive sentences.
  *People **use** a keyboard to type in information.* (active)
  *A keyboard **is used** to type in information.* (passive)
The passive is made using the verb **be** and the **past participle**. It can be used in all verb tenses.

2 Find some examples of passive sentences in the text about computers on pages 121 and 122 to 123.

3 Write passive sentences. Use the words in brackets.

(information/put/into the computer)

Information is put into the computer.

(a) (a mouse/move/around the desk)
(b) (computers/use/for thousands of jobs in the modern world)
(c) (the Internet/use/to get information from other computers)
(d) (messages/send/quickly with e-mail)
(e) (this computer/made/in Japan)
(f) (this book/write/on a computer)

4 Look.

Choose an active or passive sentence to start the sentence with the thing or person the sentence is about.

You can use a computer to do difficult calculations. (active: about what you do)
Computers can be used to do difficult calculations. (passive: about computers)

5 Write active and passive sentences. Show which are active and which are passive.

Ugo's party/organise/her school friends

Ugo's party was organised by her school friends. (passive)
Her school friends organised Ugo's party. (active)

(a) scientists/ use/computers
(b) *A man of the people*/write/Chinua Achebe
(c) The picture/take/a good photographer
(d) The gun/find/the police/yesterday
(e) My father's car/steal/a thief/last week
(f) The end-of-year exam/take/the students/next week.

Fun box

Try to answer these riddles.

- What has a face, two hands and goes round?
- What did the small hand on the clock say to the big hand?
- What does everyone in the world do at the same time?

F Speech

1 Be silent for one minute. Listen to all the sounds around you. Then write down the sounds that you heard.

2 Read this poem aloud.

Sounds of School *by* Timothy Hearn

The footsteps of a running boy,
The rumble of traffic,
The deep voice of a teacher,
The babble of voices from another classroom,
The creak of a desk,
The click as a pen or pencil is put down on a desk,
The slither of paper, sliding across a desk,
The high-pitched sound of chalk being used on a chalkboard.

3 Write a poem about the sounds in your classroom. Work in pairs.

4 Read your poem to the class.

5 Talk for one minute on 'My future career'.

   • Decide what job you would like to do when you leave school.
   • Think about the reasons why you like this job.
   • Start your talk: *When I leave school, I am going to be …*

G Dictation

Look at the words below. They are all in the dictation you are going to do. Then listen to your teacher and write the paragraph.

handheld
headset
gloves
attached
pictures
sounds
virtual reality

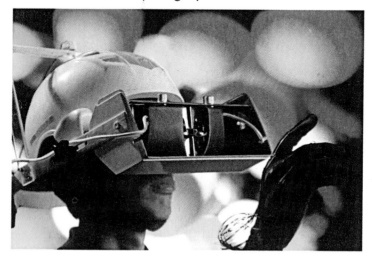

H Composition

1 Write about your future career. Explain what job you want to do, and why.

2 Write a letter to the head teacher of your school. Make a case for why the school needs to have more computers. Remember to use the layout of a formal letter.

28 A letter of condolence

A Reading 1

Before reading: Do you know anyone who has died? How did you feel?

Sakiru, Zarat, Tunde and Ugo are all in the same class at school. One Monday morning their teacher, Mr Akande, arrived late. This was very unusual. The children knew something must be wrong. When he came in, he looked sad. He asked them to read their English textbook passage quietly. He sat at his desk and held his head in his hands with his elbows resting on the desk.

After a few minutes, Tunde walked up to him and asked, "Sir, are you OK?"

Mr Akande looked up. His eyes were red and he looked sad. "No, I'm not," he replied sadly. "I lost my mother on Friday night."

"I'm very sorry to hear that, Sir," said Tunde.

As they talked, the headmistress walked in and took over the class. Mr Akande went home. Mrs Omali explained to the class what had happened. She also told them that their teacher was going to be away for five days because he needed time to prepare his mother's funeral.

During break-time, Tunde told his friends about how he felt when his dog died. He reached inside his pocket and brought out a picture.

"This is a picture of Lucky, my dog," he said.

"He was lovely!" exclaimed Zarat.

"I miss him. I was very sad when he fell ill and died," said Tunde.

"Every living thing must die," said Sakiru.

"My mother told me that but I still feel sad about it," Tunde said.

"My grandmother died last year," said Ugo.

"You must have been very upset," said Zarat.

"Yes, I cried a lot. Dad told me that because she was old, her body got tired. In the end it stopped working because no medicine could make her well again," said Ugo.

"Whatever the cause of death, people who were close to the person who has died will often feel miserable. I felt very sad when my friend died in a road accident," said Zarat.

126

B Comprehension 1

1 What was unusual that Monday morning?
2 What did Mr Akande do while the children were reading?
3 Why do you think Mr Akande's eyes were red?
4 What had happened?
5 Why did Mr Akande go home?
6 Who has Ugo lost that she loved?
7 Who has Zarat lost that she loved?
8 How did the children feel when they lost their loved ones?

C Reading 2

Before reading: What is a letter of condolence? Have you ever written one?

"Mr Akande must be feeling very unhappy," said Tunde.

"What can we do to make him feel better?" asked Ugo.

"I know, let's write him a letter of condolence," said Sakiru.

"That's a good idea!" said Tunde.

The children got together in their classroom and wrote the letter.

> Class 6 Blue
> St Louis Primary School
>
> 13 May, 20___
>
> Dear Mr Akande,
>
> We were all very sorry to hear that your mother has passed away. It must have been a terrible shock. Please know that our thoughts are with you at this difficult time. We all care about how you must feel. We hope that you can remember the good times you shared with her.
>
> We know that our letter will not make the sad or difficult feelings go away but it might help to make you feel better.
>
> May her soul rest in peace.
>
> Yours sincerely,
>
> Sakiru, **Tunde**, Ugo and Zarat

The children delivered their letter to Mrs Omali. She was very happy that they had thought of a way to make their teacher feel better. She promised to deliver the letter to Mr Akande after school.

The children were happy to know that their letter would make their teacher feel better.

D Comprehension 2

1 What did Sakiru suggest the children did for Mr Akande?

2 '... your mother has passed away.' This means
  A she has walked away,   B she has been buried,
  C she has died.

3 The children wrote the letter because
  A they wanted to help Mr Akande,
  B they wanted him to come back to school,
  C they wanted to think about Mr Akande's mother.

4 The children delivered their letter to Mrs Omali. This means
  A they posted the letter to her,   B they read the letter to her,
  C they took the letter to her.

5 What did Mrs Omali think about the letter?

6 What did Mrs Omali decide to do with the letter?

Word focus 🔍

Make sentences with these words:

funeral   upset   condolence   whatever   miserable   pass away
soul   deliver

E Grammar

1 Look.

This is how we talk about the quantity of things with countable and uncountable nouns.

Countable nouns	Uncountable nouns
no tomatoes	*no rice*
a tomato/one tomato	*– (can't be used with **a** or numbers)*
not many tomatoes	*not much rice*
a few/both tomatoes	*a little rice*
some tomatoes	*some rice*
lots of/a lot of tomatoes	*lots of/a lot of rice*

2 Play a game of 'Noughts and crosses' in two teams, A and B. Draw a grid like this.

much	some	both
not much	many	lots of
a little	any	a few

- Team A chooses a square from the grid and has to make a correct sentence using the word (or words) in the square. They must do this in no more than one minute.
- If the sentence is correct, team A can write a large nought (0) on the square. It is now team A's square.
- Team B now has a turn in the same way. If their sentence is correct, they write a large cross (X) on the square.
- The winner is the team that makes a straight line of three crosses or noughts.

3 Write *ten* sentences about yourself, your family, your school and Nigeria. Use at least one of the words from the box in each sentence. You must use all of the words at least once.

both	all	neither	none	some	any	each	many	much
too	enough	a few	few	a little	a lot of			

F Speech

Ask and answer about the people.

What does	he / she	look like?

What about	his / her	face? eyes? hair? skin colour? ...?

He She	is	tall. short. medium-height.

His Her	hair is	long. short. straight. plaited.

He She	is	slim. small. well-built.

His Her	face is	long. round.

He She	has (a)	small big	eyes. ears. nose.

His Her	skin colour is	dark. fair.

G Dictation

Look at the words above. Some of them are in the dictation you are going to do. Then listen to your teacher and write the paragraph.

H Composition

1 Look.

When you write a composition, remember the following.

* Organise your writing into paragraphs. Each paragraph should be about one idea.
* Make your opening paragraph interesting. It should show what your composition is about.
* A story must have a beginning, a middle and an end.
* A story should also have a setting, characters and a plot.
* Letters must include your address, Dear …, etc. Informal and formal letters have a different layout.
* Choose the correct style for the purpose and audience. Think about how formal your language needs to be.
* Some compositions should include only facts. Others can include your own ideas, thoughts and feelings.
* Edit and revise your writing. Make sure you have used correct spelling and punctuation. Use a dictionary if necessary.

2 Write the first paragraph of each of the following compositions.

(a) A letter of condolence to an adult who has lost his/her grandmother.

(b) A letter to a friend who has broken her leg in an accident.

(c) A story about a dog called Lucky.

(d) A description of your best friend.

(e) A report of a school event.

(f) A composition about the importance of computers in Nigeria.

29 Monkey's heart

A Reading 1

Before reading: What do you know about monkeys? Do you know any stories about monkeys?

This is a story of friendship and betrayal, cleverness and stupidity. It starts in a huge tree that grew on the seashore. Half of its branches hung over the land and the other half over the sea. And in the tree lived Monkey.

Shark lived in the sea. Sharks usually eat meat and fishermen fear the hungry shark. However, one day, Monkey threw some fruit into the sea and Shark ate it.

"Thank you, friend Monkey," said Shark, "I only have fish to eat in the sea, and I like your fruit very much."

Monkey was happy to be Shark's friend and threw fruit into the sea every morning.

One day, Shark said to Monkey, "You're so good to me that I want to do something good for you. I want to show you my home and introduce you to my brothers and sisters. I'm sure you'll get on well."

Monkey thought, "The day's very hot. It'll be nice in the water. I think I'll go."

So Monkey sat on Shark's back and off they went.

At first, Monkey was afraid but he soon got used to being under water. He stared in fascination at this new world of the fish. It was so beautiful!

"Do you like the sea?" asked Shark. "Is the sea better than your forest?"

"It's not better, but it's certainly wonderful," replied Monkey. "How far do we have to go?" he asked.

"It's not very far," Shark answered. "But now I must tell you something. Our chief, the biggest shark in the sea, is very ill. Our doctor told him that he must eat a monkey's heart to get well again. So I'm taking you to him, but I'm warning you because you're my friend."

B Comprehension 1

1 Why do fishermen fear sharks?
2 How did Monkey and Shark become friends?
3 'I'm sure you'll get on well.' This means
   A I know they will like you,   B I know they will eat you,
   C I know you will like each other.
4 What reason did Shark give for inviting Monkey to his home?
5 What was the real reason for the invitation?
6 Why did Monkey accept the invitation?
7 Why must the chief shark eat a monkey's heart?
8 'It's not better, but it's certainly wonderful'. This means
   A Monkey likes the forest but he also likes the sea,
   B Monkey likes the forest but doesn't like the sea,
   C Monkey prefers the sea because it is wonderful.

C Reading 2

Before reading: What do you think will happen? What will Monkey do?

Poor Monkey was horrified when he heard Shark's words but he did not panic. He thought hard and, as he was clever, he soon thought of a plan.

He said to Shark, "How silly you are! Why didn't you tell me that before? I don't have my heart with me. It's at home in the branches of the big tree. We monkeys always hide our hearts in the branches of trees in the daytime. We take our hearts only at night. What will you do if your chief finds that I have no heart? How angry he'll be! I'm ready to give my heart to your chief because I'm your friend, but how can I do that if I have no heart with me?"

Shark thought for a moment and then asked Monkey, "If I take you back to your tree, will you go and get your heart?"

"Of course I will, and let's go quickly. Your dear chief must not wait!" answered clever Monkey.

When they arrived back at the tree, Monkey leaped up into it saying, "Wait for me! Wait for me! I'll get my heart!"

Of course, Monkey did not come back. Shark was swimming and swimming in the water under the tree. Then he shouted, "Friend Monkey, where are you?"

Monkey began to laugh. "Do you think I'm a fool? Do you think I want to give my heart to your big hungry chief and die for him?"

"But you said your heart was in the branches of the tree," said silly Shark.

"My heart is in its place in my body. It's where it always is!" said Monkey. "And you go away! We're not friends any more!"

And with those words, Monkey threw a heavy coconut at Shark's nose.

D Comprehension 2

1 What was Monkey's plan to save his life?
2 What is the setting of the story?
3 Who are the characters?
4 Complete these sentences to make a summary of the plot.

 Monkey lived in a tree by the sea.

(a) Monkey threw some fruit into the sea, which ...

(b) One day, Shark invited ...   (c) Monkey enjoyed the journey ...

(d) Shark told Monkey that ...   (e) Monkey quickly thought ...

(f) He told Shark that ...   (g) Shark took him back ...

(h) Monkey escaped ...   (i) Shark waited for Monkey but ...

Word focus

Make sentences with these words:

betrayal   get on   warn   horrify   panic   any more

E Grammar

1 The sentence below from the story is in reported speech. Write the words that the doctor said.

 'Our doctor told him that he must eat a monkey's heart to get well again.'

2 Write the sentences from the story in reported speech.

(a) Shark said to Monkey, "I only have fish to eat in the sea, and I like your fruit very much."

(b) Monkey said to himself, "The day's very hot. It'll be nice in the water. I think I'll go."

(c) Shark asked Monkey, "Do you like the sea? Is the sea better than your forest?"

3 In the story, there are two questions using the first conditional (If + will). Write answers to the questions.

(a) *Monkey:* What will you do if your chief finds that I have no heart?
  Shark: If my chief finds out ... , he ...

(b) *Shark:*   If I take you back to your tree, will you go and get your heart?"
  Monkey: Yes, if you ..., I ...

4 'This is a story of … cleverness and stupidity.'

> **Clever** and **stupid** are adjectives. The suffixes **-ness** and **-ity** change the adjectives to nouns.

   (a) Think of *two* more adjectives which take the suffix **-ness** to become nouns.

   (b) Think of *two* more adjectives which take the suffix **-ity** to become nouns.

5 'Poor Monkey **was horrified** …'. The verb tense is the past simple passive. The verb is 'horrify'. Make sentences to show the meaning of other words in the same word family. Use a dictionary, if necessary.

   (a) horrify   (b) horror   (c) horrible   (d) horribly

6 'I'm sure you'll **get on** well.' 'Get on' is a phrasal verb. Write a sentence for each of these phrasal verbs to show their meaning. Use a dictionary.

   (a) get up   (b) get down   (c) get back   (d) get out

   (e) get around   (f) get away   (g) get over   (h) get through

7 '… he must eat a monkey's heart to get well again'. 'Must' is a modal verb. Which of the sentences below are correct and which are incorrect?

> The **modal verbs** are:
>
>   *can, could, may, might, shall, should, will, would, must, ought to.*
> - They are used before other verbs, in question-tags and in short answers.
> - They are followed by a verb in the base form.
>   *You must go now.*   *I can use a computer.*
> - Modal verbs don't change their form.
>   I often visit my aunt.   She often visits her aunt.
>   *I might visit my aunt.*   *She might visit her aunt.*
> - They make questions and negatives without using the verb **do.**
>   Sharks swim.   *Sharks can swim.*
>   Do sharks swim?   *Can sharks swim?*
>   Monkeys don't swim.   *Monkeys can't swim.*

    Monkeys can climb trees.   correct

    Tunde cans climb trees.   incorrect

   (a) It mights rain tomorrow.

   (b) Ugo can to run very fast.

   (c) They will return tomorrow.

   (d) I don't should stay here.

   (e) Would you like a drink?

   (f) I would swim under the water if I could.

F Speech

1 Look at the pictures and make up a story of 'The two oxen and the lion'. Work in groups of four. Decide what the animals are saying in each picture.

2 Act out the story. One of you is the white ox, one the black ox and one the lion. The other person is the director who will tell the actors what to do.

G Dictation

Look at the words below. They are all in the dictation you are going to do. Then listen to your teacher and write the paragraph.

| perform | costume | scenery | prop | actor | stage | sword | knife |

H Composition

1 Write your play of 'The two oxen and the lion'. Look back to Module 9, pages 40 to 42, to see what a written drama looks like.

(a) List the characters and include the stage directions.

(b) Present the conversation like this:

WHITE OX: Life is good when you have a friend.

2 Edit and revise your play.

30 Revision C

A Reading

Before reading: If you could fly, what would you do?

Wings *by* Pie Corbett

If I had wings
   I would touch the fingertips of clouds
     and glide on the wind's breath.
If I had wings
   I would taste a chunk of the sun
     as hot as peppered curry.
If I had wings
   I would listen to the clouds of sheep bleat
     that graze on the blue.
If I had wings
   I would breathe deep and sniff
     the scent of raindrops.
If I had wings
   I would gaze at the people
     who cling to the earth's crust.
If I had wings
   I would dream of
     swimming the deserts
       and walking the seas.

B Comprehension

1 Find words in the poem which mean
  (a) to move slowly and easily,
  (b) a piece,
  (c) the noise a sheep makes,
  (d) to eat growing grass,
  (e) to suck in air through the nose to smell something,
  (f) a pleasant smell,
  (g) stare,
  (h) a hard outside surface.

2 Recite the poem.

3 Write another verse for the poem. Start: If I had wings
                         I would . . .

C Reading quiz

1 Find the answers in the Reading texts in Modules 21 to 29.
   (a) When the children organised the birthday party (Module 21), who planned the party games?
   (b) Why did Mallam Kolo receive a gift at the prize-giving ceremony?
   (c) Who gave the St Louis Primary School 100,000 Naira?
   (d) Who recognised the twins when they returned to the village of Serki?
   (e) Where was 'Zik' born?
   (f) How old was 'Zik' when he died?
   (g) Who wrote the story, *Shaihu Umar*?
   (h) When was Nelson Mandela born?
   (i) Which part of a computer system looks like a TV?
   (j) When do you write someone a letter of condolence?

2 Write *ten* questions of your own about the Reading texts in Modules 21 to 29.

3 Ask your questions.

> **Word focus**   Make sentences with these words:
> decorate   reliable   exile   recognise   obey   waist   nervously
> complicated   disappear   miserable

D Grammar

Which word or phrase (A to E) is the most nearly opposite in meaning to the underlined word?

1 People often think that computers are underlined{complicated}.
   A simple   B difficult   C cheap   D reliable   E unreliable

2 I like stories set in ancient times.
   A new   B old   C modern   D history   E late

3 This is a story about cleverness.
   A stupid   B stupidly   C stupor   D stupidity   E stupidness

Which word or phrase (A to E) is nearest in meaning to the underlined word?

4 The proprietor of the school is on holiday.
   A leader   B chairman   C cleaner   D owner   E head teacher

5 The flood was a great misfortune.
   A accident   B happening   C disaster   D earthquake   E loss of money

6 These parents are reliable.
   A kind   B happy   C generous   D punctual   E responsible

Which sentence (A to E) explains the meaning of the sentence best?

7 To err is human.
   A Humans mustn't make mistakes.   B Mistakes are errors.
   C It is normal to make mistakes.   D Humans are mistakes.
   E Humans must make mistakes.

8 This soup is too salty for me.
   A The soup is very salty in my opinion.   B I don't like salt in soup.
   C I can't eat salt in soup.   D I like the soup.
   E I can't eat the soup because of the salt.

9 If I had seen you before, I would have given you the book.
   A I gave you the book when I saw you.
   B I will give you the book when I see you.
   C I haven't given you the book because I haven't seen you.
   D I haven't given you the book because I don't want to.
   E I wanted to give you the book but I don't want to now.

Which of the questions (A to E) is the one which the sentence answers?

10 It's Ugo's.
   A Is this Ugo's?   B Where is Ugo?   C Whose is this?
   D Who is Ugo?   E It's Ugo's, isn't it?

11 We haven't got any.
   A What shall we cook?   B Whose is this rice?   C What is this?
   D Where is the rice?   E Have we got any rice?

12 Yes, I did.
   A I saw you, didn't I?   B You saw her, didn't you?
   C Where was she?   D You won't see her, will you?
   E You like her, don't you?

Choose the words (A to E) which best fill the gaps in the paragraph.

In a library there is often a section ___13___ biographical and autobiographical
books. A biography is the story of someone's ___14___ . An autobiography is the
story of your ___15___ life. Most famous or successful people don't ___16___ time to
write their own story so a ___17___ does this.
   A have   B life   C own   D of   E biographer

Complete the sentences. Choose the word or words that best fill the gap.

18 You can't go to secondary school _____ you have been to primary school.
   A if   B unless   C when   D except   E because

19 My father drives a car _____ than my mother.
   A faster   B more faster   C fast   D more faster   E fastest

20 Zarat found the money, _____ she?
   A found   B did   C didn't   D isn't   E wasn't

E Speech

1 Perform the play you wrote in Module 29.

2 Give a short speech on *one* of the following topics.

    (a) Me   (b) My family

    (c) My best friend   (d) My home

    (e) My life at primary school   (f) My future life at secondary school

    (g) A famous Nigerian   (h) Computers

3 Which is your favourite poem in this book? (Use the Contents page at the beginning to help you find all the poems.) Recite it to the class.

F Dictation

Listen to your teacher and write the paragraph.

G Composition

Choose *one* of the following to write. Don't forget to edit and revise what you write.

    (a) A story called 'Wings'.

    (b) A letter to a penfriend in another country to tell him/her about your school.

    (c) A letter to your head teacher to explain your plans for the future. You can ask for any help you need.

    (d) A factual report about what happened between the two oxen and the lion.

    (e) A page of Monkey's diary for the day he went away with Shark.

Appendix: Irregular verbs

Base form	Simple past	Past participle	Base form	Simple past	Past participle
become	became	become	hit	hit	hit
begin	began	begun	hold	held	held
bend	bent	bent	hurt	hurt	hurt
bite	bit	bitten	keep	kept	kept
bleed	bled	bled	kneel	knelt	knelt
blow	blew	blown	know	knew	known
break	broke	broken	lay	laid	laid
bring	brought	brought	leave	left	left
build	built	built	let	let	let
burst	burst	burst	lie	lay	lain
buy	bought	bought	lose	lost	lost
catch	caught	caught	make	made	made
choose	chose	chosen	mean	meant	meant
come	came	come	pay	paid	paid
cost	cost	cost	put	put	put
cut	cut	cut	read	read	read
dig	dug	dug	ride	rode	ridden
do	did	done	ring	rang	rung
draw	drew	drawn	rise	rose	risen
drink	drank	drunk	run	ran	run
drive	drove	driven	say	said	said
eat	ate	eaten	see	saw	seen
fall	fell	fallen	sell	sold	sold
feed	fed	fed	set	set	set
feel	felt	felt	shake	shook	shaken
fight	fought	fought	shoot	shot	shot
find	found	found	shut	shut	shut
fly	flew	flown	sing	sang	sung
forget	forgot	forgotten	sink	sank	sunk
freeze	froze	frozen	sit	sat	sat
get	got	got	speak	spoke	spoken
give	gave	given	spend	spent	spent
go	went	gone	spread	spread	spread
grow	grew	grown	stand	stood	stood
hang	hung	hung	steal	stole	stolen
have	had	had	stick	stuck	stuck
hear	heard	heard	sting	stung	stung
hide	hid	hidden	swim	swam	swum

140

Base form	Simple past	Past participle	Base form	Simple past	Past participle
take	took	taken	upset	upset	upset
teach	taught	taught	wake	woke	woken
tear	tore	torn	wear	wore	worn
tell	told	told	win	won	won
think	thought	thought	write	wrote	written
throw	threw	thrown			

The verbs **be** and **have** are very irregular. Here are their full forms:

be

Simple present: I am
You are
He is
She is
It is
We are
You are
They are

Simple past: I was
You were
He was
She was
It was
We were
You were
They were

Present participle: being

Past participle: been

have

Simple present: I have
You have
He has
She has
It has
We have
You have
They have

Simple past: I had
You had
He had
She had
It had
We had
You had
They had

Present participle: having

Past participle: had

Word list

A
abandon
academic
accused
actor
addict
advantage
alcohol
amazement
ancestor
ancient
antonym
appoint
appropriate
arrest
ashtray
athletics
attach
attention
audience
autobiography

B
babble
bacteria
ban
bang
baptise
baton
batter
beat
benefit
betrayal
beware
bill
biography
biology
bitter
blanket
bleat
block out
break down
bronze
broth
build up
Bunsen burner
burst open

C
caffeine
calculation
camera
cast
castle
chapter
charcoal
chart
chemicals
chemistry
chisel
chlorine
cholera
chunk
civilised
come across
complain
complete
complicated
conditions
condolence
confident
conservation
consonant
container
contents page
continent
costume
courage
court
crackle
craft
crate
creak
creature
criticise
crowded
crust
culture
cure
curry

D
damage
data
deal
decorate
decrease
deliver
department
desalination
desert
destination
development
diagram
dialogue
director
disadvantage
disappear
disaster
discipline
discover
disease
district
disturb
divide
dozen
draft
dramatic
drawbacks
drift
drip
drive away
dysentery

E
editor
elder
elect
e-mail
enemy
entry
equipment
erect
event
evidence
exile
experience
experiment
explode
explore
extinct
extracurricular
eyelid

F
factory
fascinating
fertile
fiery
filter
fin
fine(n)
flap
flask
float
flow
fluid
flush
foreign
forgive
found
frequently
fuel
furthermore

G
gain
gaze
gecko
generous
germs
get on
ghost
gills
glide
glitter
gold
government
grab
gradually
granted
grapes
gratefully
gravel
graze
groan
guilty
gush

H
handheld
harm
hatchet
headline
headquarters
headset
helmet
heroine
high-pitched
HIV/AIDS
honour
horrify
hover

human
hurdles

I
identical
idiom
illegal
illustrate
incident
increase
index
influence
injury
innocent
Internet

J
journalist
jury

K
keyboard

L
lack of
law
leader
level

M
magazine
magistrate
mankind
marine
Master of
  Ceremonies
measles
medal
mend
merchant
mess
military
military coup
miserable
misfortune
misuse
modern
monitor
murmur

N
nervously
nicotine
nip
nonsense
nowadays

O
obey
observe

occur
operate
opportunity
organ
originally
otherwise
overtake
oxygen

P
pace
package
pads
parasol
pass away
payment
perform
personally
petrol
photographer
physics
plot
poke
polio
politician
polling station
popular
population
praise
professor
program
pronunciation
proof reading
prop
proprietor
protect
protection
proverb
publicise
publish
puddle
puff

Q
quality
quarrel

R
receipt
receptionist
recognise
reference
regularly
rehearse
relay
reliable
reluctantly

reporter
represent
request
require
rescue
resident
responsibly
rib
rival
roller blades
rolling
Romans
rumble

S
sailing ship
sale
sample
savannah
scale
scarce
scenery
scent
scratch
section
sentence
servant
service
setting
shade
shame
shark
shave
shoelace
shrine
shy
silver
skeleton
slide projector
slither
snatch
sniff
solution
soul
souvenir
sparks
spend
stage
statue
steadily
steering wheel
stray
strict
stroke
stumble

style
suitable
surface
surrounding
sword
symbol
synonym
systems unit

T
test tube
theatre
thesaurus
tickle
tip
tobacco
tourism
trap
trip
trophy
troublemaker
truth
twins

U
unconscious
unfortunately
unite

V
vaccine
valley
version
violent
virtual reality
virus
volunteer
vote
vowel

W
waist
ward
warn
wealth
well-built
whale
whatever
whooping cough
wildlife
wine
witness
wonder
wrap

Macmillan Education
Between Towns Road, Oxford, OX4 3PP
A division of Macmillan Publishers Limited
Companies and representatives throughout the world

www.macmillan-africa.com

ISBN 978-9780-18338-7

Designed by Kamae Design
Illustrated by Sarah Wimperis, GCI
Cover design by Macmillan Publishers Limited
Cover illustration by Sarah Wimperis

We would like to thank the following schools for their participation
in the development of this course:
Eduland Children's School, Lagos
High Tree International School, Lagos
Oluyole Private School, Ibadan
Richmab International School, Ibadan
First Choice Children School, Owerri
Premier International School, Kano

We would like to acknowledge Catherine Adenle for her
contribution to the development of the reading passages
in the following Modules: 7, 8, 9, 13, 15, 16, 21, 22, 24, 26 and 28

The authors and publishers would like to thank the following for
permission to reproduce their material:
Little, Brown/Nolwazi for the extract from A Long Walk to Freedom by Nelson Mandela; Walker Books for
the poem 'Fire' from Out & About by Shirley Hughes; Random House Group Limited for 'Penfriend' and
'Sleep' from Singing Down the Breadfruit by Pauline Stewart, published by Red Fox

If any copyright holder have been omitted, please contact the publishers who will make the necessary
arrangements at the first opportunity.

The authors and publishers would like to thank the following for
permission to reproduce their photographs:
African Pictures.Net: Darren Humphreys – iafrika p.5 (brt); Juda Ngwenya p.37 (l); Dave Richardson –
iafrika p.139. Alamy: Gary Cook p.4; Tim Graham p.5 (bc); Giles Moberly p.5 (bl); David Wall p.5 (brb);
David Lyons p.37 (r); Popperfoto p.110; Tom Spalding p.111 (tr). Corbis: p.5 (t); Smalles Alex p.69;
Bettmann pp.107, 108; Reuters p.111 (bl); Peter Turnley pp.112 (c), 115; David Turnley p.112 (r); Getty
Images pp.65, 112 (l), 121, 125

Printed and bound in Malaysia
2009   2008
10 9   8